A PLUME BOOK

THE GEOGRAPHY OF WINE

BRIAN J. SOMMERS is a member of the Department of Geography at Central Connecticut University, where he is a professor of geography and Assistant to the Dean of Arts and Sciences. He has taught the geography of wine for many years.

THE GEOGRAPHY
OF

Wine

HOW LANDSCAPES, CULTURES,
TERROIR, AND THE WEATHER
MAKE A GOOD DROP

BRIAN J. SOMMERS

A PLUME BOOK

PLUME
Published by the Penguin Group
Penguin Group (USA) Inc., 375 Hudson Street, New York, New York 10014,
U.S.A. • Penguin Group (Canada), 90 Eglinton Avenue East, Suite 700,
Toronto, Ontario, Canada M4P 2Y3 (a division of Pearson Penguin Canada
Inc.) • Penguin Books Ltd., 80 Strand, London WC2R 0RL, England •
Penguin Ireland, 25 St. Stephen's Green, Dublin 2, Ireland (a division of Penguin
Books Ltd.) • Penguin Group (Australia), 250 Camberwell Road, Camberwell,
Victoria 3124, Australia (a division of Pearson Australia Group Pty. Ltd.) •
Penguin Books India Pvt. Ltd., 11 Community Centre, Panchsheel Park,
New Delhi – 110 017, India • Penguin Group (NZ), 67 Apollo Drive,
Rosedale 0632, Auckland, New Zealand (a division of Pearson New Zealand
Ltd.) • Penguin Books (South Africa) (Pty.) Ltd., 24 Sturdee Avenue,
Rosebank, Johannesburg 2196, South Africa

Penguin Books Ltd., Registered Offices: 80 Strand, London WC2R 0RL, England

First published by Plume, a member of Penguin Group (USA) Inc.

First Printing, March 2008
10 9 8 7 6 5 4 3 2 1

Ⓟ REGISTERED TRADEMARK—MARCA REGISTRADA

LIBRARY OF CONGRESS CATALOGING-IN-PUBLICATION DATA

Sommers, Brian J.
    The geography of wine : how landscapes, cultures, terroir, and the weather make a
good drop / Brian J. Sommers.
        p.   cm.
    Includes index.
    ISBN 978-0-452-28890-4
1. Wine and wine making.   2. Viticulture.   I. Title.
    TP548.S689 2008
    641.2'2—dc22   2007035417

Printed in the United States of America
Set in Adobe Garamond
Designed by Eve L. Kirch

This book is dedicated to Betsy, Max, and Nate. Their patience and understanding were instrumental in its publication. This book is also dedicated to John Dome whose inspiration led me down this path.

CONTENTS

THE GEOGRAPHY

OF

GEOGRAPHY AND THE
STUDY OF WINE

Wine is more than taste and smell and appearance. There is a great deal of science and artistry in each bottle of wine you drink. What I hope you will come to appreciate in the chapters that follow is that behind the science and the artistry is geography. As geography tends to be a poorly understood subject, few may recognize its proximity or importance to wine. But it is possible to see and even taste its influence.

Most people think that geographers memorize place names and, well, not much else. Thankfully, that is not what it is all about. Geography is a science of space. And as in all sciences our goal is to explain why. We answer *why* things are where they are. There is a heck of a lot of good geography behind every bottle of wine. My goal is to make you aware of that geography and to convey some of the fun in deepening one's understanding of it.

So what does geography bring to a wine party? It can answer some of the questions that you may already have about wine. Why is Bordeaux a great place for red wines? Why do some places produce Rieslings and others produce chardonnay? How did wine production end up in (pick your favorite region)? How does wine allow us to taste a place? These are the kinds of questions we can answer through geography. So if you are interested in these kinds of questions, you may be a geographer without even knowing it.

There are books on the history of wine, on the tasting of wine, on the quality of and value of vintages, on the wines of specific regions, on growing grapes, on winemaking, and on cooking with wine. There are wine books for idiots, wine atlases, and vineyard photo essays. This book does not compete with any of these. This book is an introduction to the geographic principles that provide a greater understanding of wine. It is a good accompaniment to all of those other wine books that you have on your shelf.

Wine is a fertile ground for the science of geography. This is why viticulture and wine find their way into even introductory geography texts and why courses in the geography of wine appear in colleges throughout North America. Geographers tend to think either in terms of themes or of places. In the world of wine, people think of wine regions and what makes them tick. People who think thematically consider how climate, geology, biology, culture, politics, and economics affect wine and how the geographies that relate to these factors have an impact on wine regions. In this book you will see that I am very much a representative of the thematic way of thinking.

A thematic approach complements all the great regional wine books that are out there. Their text and photographs tell us in vivid detail about the places that produce great wine. Each chapter in this book provides a glimpse into the geography that makes those places great. That is not to say that the regional approach is excluded. The regional close-ups at the end of each chapter are important for demonstrating concepts discussed in the chapter. For example, Mosel vineyards are great examples of how microclimates affect winemaking, and South Africa and Chile illustrate the links between colonialism and wine.

• • •

I would like to be able to say that my interest in wine dates back to the summer of 1986, when I spent a month working at an archeological dig in the French Alps. Unfortunately I can't do that. I was blissfully ignorant of the world of wine even though it was all around me. Instead of indulging in the local wines, we drank cheap generic beer. I always try to muster up excuses. I was young and stupid. I was poor. I was led astray by the other American students who were working the dig. There are all sorts of possible explanations. But I cannot blame the villagers who lived around the dig. They were great. They shared their local wines and foods with us every chance that they could. What can I say? It is the curse of youth. Back then we did not realize that drinking generic beer was hazardous to our taste buds.

My interest in wine actually stems from my first semester as a graduate student in the Geography Department at Miami University. Most voyages of wine discovery do not begin in Oxford, Ohio. Mine did, thanks to John Dome. John had been teaching a course called the Geography of Wine at Miami for decades when I first met him. The course drew a regular crowd of locals and large numbers of business majors who saw it as a means of social advancement. I was assigned to the class as John's graduate assistant.

I thought at first that the whole thing was a lark. I learned that you do not chill red wine—after I had chilled it, of course. I also learned how to use a corkscrew without filling the bottle with little bits of cork (admittedly that took me a while). Twice a week I would do the setup, listen to the lectures, and watch the slides. I would end the evenings by cleaning up and taking home any unopened bottles. By the end of the course I had a kitchen full of wine bottles. I learned a bit about which foods go with wine, although I never did find a good match for Fritos. But, more than anything, I had an appreciation for the fact that there was a heck of a lot of geography in wine. It was also the point at which I began to really regret the days I spent swilling generic beer in the Alps.

People who are not geographers and who have never taken a course in the subject are often at a complete loss to explain what geography is. So you may be reading this, perhaps over a nice glass of wine, and wondering what geography has to do with that wonderful taste. Or you may be thinking that the remainder of the book will be lists of wine regions and the wines that they produce. First, please understand that I am not an expert on those kinds of details. I am also not a good wine taster. I could spend a very happy lifetime in a world of twelve-dollar bottles of wine. So what can I contribute?

Geography is a way to understand how something works. To a geographer, wine is an intricate puzzle. Some people can look at a pile of parts and see how they all fit together to form a car. Others can look at a Web page and visualize the HTML code. We look at the world around us and try to figure out how it works. So if you have ever wondered why some places produce chardonnay while others produce pinot noir, why Chile is the largest wine producer in South America, why some vineyards have soil that resembles a gravel driveway, why the Europeans often name their wines after the places where they are produced, or why vineyards and wineries in one place look different from those in another, then you are asking questions a geographer might ask. More important, they are questions a geographer can answer.

Geography is in every drop of wine we drink. But is wine in every bit of geography? If you look at how we study geography, the answer is yes. The fact of the matter is that there are many ways in which geographers approach their subject matter and wine can fit into all of them. In 1964 William Pattison wrote a seminal article for the *Journal of Geography*. In it Pattison broke down the breadth and history of geographic study into the traditions of environmental studies, man–land study (sometimes called human ecology), regional study, and spatial analysis. Even today, these are the four basic approaches that geographers take toward their subject. Wine fits nicely into all of them.

The environmental tradition is where geography intersects with the "natural" sciences: physics, chemistry, geology, and biology. If you asked geographers from this tradition how he or she would study wine, what you would get in return is an answer based heavily on concepts of environmental science. They might talk about vintages in terms of the movement of the jet stream. They will look at grape production as it relates to heating-degree days. They will examine the influence of soil chemistry and how it affects wine taste. They will have a purely scientific approach to the subject of wine.

This would be a very different approach to that of geographers working in the man–land or human ecology tradition.

Their approach would be one of social science—regarding wine as an agricultural/industrial product, as a cultural adaptation, and as an economic activity. They will be concerned with the patterns of trade and the geographic expansion of the wine industry over time, or why a certain type of wine may be specific to a group of people. Closer to home they could even study the geographic factors that determine the success and failure of local wine retailers. And while the environmental studies and man–land traditions differ greatly, they do have one thing in common. They look at topics and relate them to places.

The "topical" approach of the environmental studies and man–land traditions is what sets them apart from the regional-studies tradition of geography. If you read Homer, you will find that there is a healthy amount of place description in his writing. The regional-studies tradition is part of a steady evolution from geography as background information, to works whose purpose is place description, to the modern regional approach of understanding the "puzzle" of what makes the geography of those places. So, rather than studying a topic, such as the expansion of the wine trade, a geographer from the regional-studies tradition would study a place and how that expansion has had an impact on it.

It is an interesting historical accident that this tradition comes to us via French geography. In the late 1800s and early 1900s French geographers, exemplified by Paul Vidal de La Blache, specialized in producing regional monographs. Students of de La Blache would spend months living in and studying a region in order to come to an understanding of how it worked. The monographs they produced are vivid historical glimpses of places that may be unrecognizable today. We can admire them for their art and imagine how satisfying it must have been to conduct such research in wine country.

The last of the four traditions of geography is the spatial-analysis tradition. Although it has its origins in early mapmaking and navigation, it has evolved into the "toolbox" of modern geography. It involves computer mapping, statistical analysis and the modeling of spatial data, the use of geographic information systems (GIS), and remote-sensing applications using satellite imagery. While the other traditions might use these tools as part of their research on the geography of wine, those versed in the spatial-analysis tradition might look at wines as an application of their tools. They might use satellite data to determine the moisture levels in vineyard soils, they could use spatial modeling techniques to predict the pathways of pest infestations, or they might apply geographic information systems to identify the lowest-cost transportation routes for getting wines to market.

The geographic study of wine is just part of a much broader academic world of wine. That world is divided into three basic areas of knowledge. First, there is the study of enology, the study of winemaking. It includes such things as the way wine is produced, the chemistry of wine, and its impact on human taste/smell and physiology. Second, there is the study of viticulture, essentially the study of grape agriculture. Universities that provide training in these fields are preparing students for employment in the industry. They are also providing assistance to grape growers and winemakers. So it should come as no surprise that universities specializing in these fields, such as the University of

California (Davis) and Cornell University, are often located near places that produce wine. The results of their labor can be found in the wines of their regions.

The third area of study is more broadly focused: the anthropology, economics, geography, history, or political science of wine and wine regions. This approach is purely for academic or personal interest. It plays no role in producing a better grape crop or a higher quality bottle of wine. It is not about making money. It is about understanding the broader context of wine. For wine lovers, this approach is all about satisfying our curiosities and adding to the experience of wine

For the most part, the academic study of wine is limited to those areas which produce wine. That is because the academic study of wine faces a significant image problem. As a society we are concerned about alcohol. This is especially true at a time when there is increasing recognition that binge drinking and alcoholism are serious problems on college campuses. Part of that image problem hinges on the view that studying a commodity of wealth is elitist. In areas that produce wine, these image problems fade in the face of the economic reality of the wine industry. Outside wine-producing regions, these image problems make those of us who study wine a bit defensive.

Even if the academic study of wine does have an image problem, as a wine enthusiast I think that it is a lot of fun. Moreover, I think that geography is a great tool for learning about and appreciating wine. The nice thing about geography is that we can easily take it out of the classroom and into the field. For the study of wine, this means visiting wineries and vineyards. Taking day trips to local vineyards is entertaining and gives us the opportunity to turn our love of wine into great learning experiences. We can take the geographic concepts that we learn in books and build on them. We may even find the experiences so rewarding that we become wine tourists; traveling to wine regions in other countries, learning about their wines, experiencing their cultures. Naturally the owners of the vineyards hope that you buy some of their wine as part of your visit. I like to rationalize such purchases as data collection.

Whether we are visiting a vineyard at home or abroad, this book will help us to ask good geographic questions when we get there. We might look to identify which grapes are being grown and in what quantities, and how soil, drainage, or climate are factors in their growth. Have these decisions been made based on market forces, on the ease of management, or on some other consideration? We might also look at the management of the vines. How are the vines trellised? Are the vines perpendicular or parallel to the slope of the land and of the incoming rays of the sun? What is the spacing of the vines? How are the spaces between the trellises being used? How are the vines being pruned? Are there any end-of-row plantings?

As wine geographers we evolve from someone who looks at a vineyard and thinks that it is attractive, to one who understands how it works. Anyone can go to a winery, take a look around, and buy some wine. In becoming scholars of wine we can talk to vintners and winemakers about their craft in an informed manner, learning more each time we do. That is the nice thing about being a wine geographer, a wine historian, or a wine chemist. We gain a deeper understanding of wine and perhaps more enjoyment out of each and every drop.

WINE LANDSCAPES
AND REGIONS

Forty years before Pattison, academic geography was dominated by the concept of "landscape." From the 1920s to the 1950s, landscapes were considered the basic building blocks for introducing geographic concepts and for thinking about the world around us. It may not be the preeminent concept it once was, but the study of landscapes still shapes geography today. For geographers landscape is not just an aesthetic. The images of vineyards that we see in photo essays of Tuscany or Provence communicate a great deal of geographic information. Seeing how it all fits together, like someone who has just finished a 1,500-piece jigsaw puzzle, is part of the fun of being a geographer.

REGIONAL GEOGRAPHY AND WINE REGIONS

Wine stores typically organize wines by their place of origin. Most of these are fairly straightforward. Australian wines are from Australia. California wines are from California. But what about the Napa Valley? What exactly is the Côte D'Or? These may be places that people recognize as being special or unique, but they might not be able to easily identify them on a map. We could say they are political jurisdictions drawn on a map, or areas economically linked to a central community, such as Napa or Beaune. But in some cases, these definitions don't work all that well. The reality is that the term "region" can be defined in a great many ways. What do we mean when we refer to Burgundy, the Willamette Valley, and Chianti as wine regions?

In the United States, what is the Midwest? The South? New England? Is Pennsylvania part of the Midwest, Northeast, or both? When we talk about regions we may or may not have nice neat political boundaries to work with. We might recognize Connecticut, Maine, Massachusetts, New Hampshire, Rhode Island, and Vermont as being "New England," but for someone in Missouri, located in the middle of the continental United States, does the term "Midwest" make any sense, considering that the Midwestern states are neither middle nor western?

Most of the major wine-producing countries have gotten past this labeling problem. Over time they have developed regional identification systems as a means of product protection and regulation. These systems define the boundaries and the identifications of wine-producing regions. They can tell us in no uncertain terms exactly what is and is not part of a specific wine region, so when we see a place label on a wine bottle it means something that is very well defined. For instance, the region may be defined by considerations of environment, or by a type of wine production that has evolved over time in that environment. Or it may be based on culture. There may be clues in the landscape that will allow us to see where Bordeaux begins and ends. We just need to become well trained at reading landscapes in order to see them.

Consider how we might look at a painting by the nineteenth-century landscape painter John Constable. We might appreciate his use of color, or the way his works bring rural life alive. His landscapes are to be looked at, appreciated, and admired. For geographers landscapes are not just things to be admired like fine art. They are to be "read" as one would read a book. Landscape is not necessarily a background for an action in the foreground. It can be the subject itself. Geographers sometimes pay too much attention to the landscape. We cannot help it; it is an occupational hazard, especially for those of us who like to watch movies. As a reader of landscapes, I can delude myself that determining where a movie was shot based on its locations is a semi-intellectual pursuit. (Yes, a rather feeble rationalization, but I'm going to stick with it.) We wait as the closing credits roll just to see where the movie was filmed.

Landscape and all of its components really do mean something. In looking at a valley of vineyards, we are looking at something that has evolved from the interplay between people and nature, where both environment and people have played a significant role in creating the "look" of the land. Photo essays of wine landscapes aren't just pretty pictures. They are sources of information waiting to be unraveled.

How Do You Read a Landscape?

In Pierce Lewis's *Axioms for Reading the Landscape*, he defines a number of rules of the road for reading landscapes. Landscapes are physical manifestations of culture and of a people. If places are similar in appearance, then in some way so are their cultures. Changes in the landscape that stand the test of time are those which are important to the people. Fads fade.

To understand a landscape according to Lewis we need to break ourselves of the habit of searching for those things that are most prominent or are unique. Something that is very common is not necessarily "boring." Rather it is something that is so important that it is present everywhere. As you drive along Interstate 87 through upstate New York's wine regions, you will pass mile after mile of vineyards that look pretty much the same. In some cases it may be only the color of the tractors (blue for Ford, red for Massey Ferguson, and green for John Deere— or so my kids tell me) that sets them apart. This similarity may eventually get a bit monotonous, but it means something that should not be overlooked.

In our first attempts at reading landscapes we need to consider that landscape elements have a place in time. They have a cultural context and an environmental context. An area that is environmentally similar to Bordeaux and was settled by the French a few hundred years ago is likely to have a landscape that appears to be much the same as Bordeaux's. We understand this intuitively. Even as children we know enough about environment and culture to recognize when things "fit" and when they don't. It is an innate geographic ability. This is not to say that reading landscapes is easy, far from it. As Lewis is quick to point out, landscapes may convey a great deal of information. That does not mean that they are obvious about it.

Once we are adept at identifying the physical features (landforms, plants, buildings, and so on) in a landscape, the next step is to begin to make sense of them. What forces are at work? What shaped the physical features that we see? Being able to answer these questions will allow us to take a very important step. It will take us from understanding the way a landscape looks to explaining *why* it looks that way.

When geographers talk about the way a landscape has been shaped—the form of the landscape—we use the term "morphology." Carl Sauer, whose important contributions dominated geographical theory for more than thirty years, made this concept prominent in his seminal work "The Morphology of Landscape" in 1925. It provided a framework for explaining the formation of landscapes. The flow chart below is a product of Sauer's work. The basic premise is that in any location there are environmental forces at work. Through time these forces create the natural forms listed. When we put the natural forms together the product is a natural landscape. That landscape will

Environmental Forces	Natural Forms	Medium	Human Forms	Produce
Geologic	Climate		Population	
Climatic	Land surface	Natural landscape	Housing	Cultural landscapes
Biotic	Soil		Religion	
	Drainage		Society	
	Resources			
	Plant and animal life			

have a climate, land surface, soil, drainage, and other features that may make it unique. Many locations will share the same sets of natural forms.

The natural landscape is the backdrop or medium for the activities of people. People alter the landscape according to their culture, needs, and interests. These alterations form the cultural landscape. As an example we can look to the landscape of the Great Plains states. Prior to the waves of Anglo settlement in the 1800s, the region was populated by nomadic tribal groups. With Anglo settlement, the tribal groups were replaced by farmers. The medium, the natural landscape, was the same in either case. Clearly, however, human impacts made the cultural landscapes quite different.

Sauer never used wine regions as a focus of his published research, but certainly his theories can be applied to wine landscapes. Consider the Napa and Sonoma regions. We can read the puzzle of the natural landscape and put the pieces together to see how they were created. We can figure out how each of those pieces was altered by the winemakers who had settled in the valleys. We can attempt to understand why people chose to make the alterations they did, and in so doing we understand the landscapes of Napa and Sonoma, or even the landscape pictured on the front cover of this book. You can try your hand at this the next time you are traveling through wine country or leafing through your favorite photographs of wine country. And do not worry if this kind of reading proves to be a bit difficult. Nobody expects you to be Sherlock Holmes right from the start. It takes study. It also takes a good deal of practice.

The concept of landscapes is being used more and more as the basis of historic and cultural preservation programs. When we think about historic preservation we tend to think about individual objects—for instance, a building, a covered bridge, or a statue. While this is all well and good, often only the unique or the special are chosen for preservation, and preserving these individual objects does not necessarily preserve the setting, which in some instances is really the most important thing. There are also those things which we find so common that preserving one of them does not do them justice. Those are the things that we often fail to recognize until they are gone. If you visit Lancaster County in Pennsylvania, try to find a landscape of intact Amish farms. It is a very difficult task, as everywhere there is development, commercialization, and the most intrusive forms of tourism.

With these ideas in mind, historic and cultural preservationists have become more involved in landscape preservation. A leader in this trend has been UNESCO. In identifying sites of importance to all mankind, UNESCO has expanded its World Heritage Sites program to include landscapes of worldwide importance. The program recognizes those landscapes of importance, but does not in itself have the ability to protect them. Rather it provides a basis for local planning and preservation of those landscapes as well as for the funding needed to do the work.

WINE, LANDSCAPE, AND *TERROIR*

When it comes to the study of wine, the morphology of landscape is very important. That is because Sauer's morphology of landscape is a geographic parallel to the study of *terroir*.

Those of you who are wine enthusiasts are probably already familiar with the term "*terroir*." You may have seen the word on wine labels, in books, or on Web pages for your favorite wines. The term is everywhere because *terroir* is a pivotal concept for understanding wine and the places it comes from.

For those of you not familiar with the concept, *terroir* is French for "ground" or "soil," but it is more than that. It is used to describe all the local features of environment and society that have an effect on wine. Many people believe that all the features of a place taken as a whole—its *terroir*—have a distinctive influence that you can taste in the wine. This is what it means to taste geography. *Terroir* tells us that place matters, which geographers have been arguing since the dawn of time. Accordingly, wine geographers love the concept. Morphology of landscape tells us that what we see in the world around us is a product of environmental forces and the decisions that people make in that environment. *Terroir* tells us also that what we taste is a product of environmental forces and the decisions that people make in that environment. So, needless to say, wine geographers swear by the concept.

Terroir is an important concept in this book. In fact, we can look at the chapters to come as snapshots of how geographers study the factors that go into *terroir*. So by the time you are done reading you will not only understand the geography of wine. You will also have a deeper understanding of *terroir* and its significance.

SAINT-EMILION

If we are looking to do a case study in the reading of a wine landscape, then we have to rely on the wealth of photography on the Internet or in your favorite wine atlas. And given UNESCO's cultural landscape preservation program, Saint-Emilion in France would make as good a case study as any. Saint-Emilion was the first wine landscape to be placed on UNESCO's cultural landscape preservation list. More than that, Saint-Emilion just looks like what we might think a wine landscape should look like.

In studying landscapes we begin with nature. While there are some localized variations in the climate, the more significant variation is in the region's geology. Saint-Emilion is positioned on the slopes where the coastal plain and the broad valleys of the Garonne and Dordogne rivers meet the foothills of the interior. It thus has two distinct *terroirs*. The plains below Saint-Emilion have alluvial soils deposited over time by the Dordogne and its tributaries. These soils are deep and gravelly. The *terroir* of the hillsides and of the plateau of Saint-Emilion is significantly different in its geology. The hills and plateau are rich in limestone. The limestone weathers easily and adds nutrients to the soil. These differences in geology mean that merlot and cabernet franc grapes grown in different communes in Saint-Emilion may have significant differences in taste.

Saint-Emilion is a little more than twenty miles east of Bordeaux and around fifty-five miles east of the Atlantic. At that distance it is far enough from the ocean to have a climate much more like that of central France. With such a climate, it is a region well suited for wines produced from merlot and cabernet franc grapes. The climate and soils of the region could be used for any number of agricultural products, but the success of viticulture has made grapes the region's single dominant crop. This sort of monoculture is not a recent occurrence. Saint-Emilion has a history of wine production that dates from Roman times, and that rivals other production areas within Bordeaux.

For geographers the one shortcoming of *terroir* is that it stops with the wine. As geographers we are interested in much more. In a place such as Saint-Emilion we would be missing a great deal of intriguing geography if we stopped with the wine. That is because there is something very special about Saint-Emilion. It is a medieval walled town, seemingly untouched by the passage of time. From its walls you can peer out across the valley of the Dordogne, and only occasionally catch glimpses of the trains running from Bordeaux into central France. The castle, town walls, churches, homes, and even the streets are made of native limestone. About the only things not made of limestone are the roofing tiles, which are fabricated from clay mined in the river valleys. The uniformity of the building materials and the historic architecture make Saint-Emilion a postcard of what we imagine a provincial French town to look like: a maze of winding streets, hidden courtyards, cafés, and churches. Some of the limestone used in the town's construction was quarried on site. This has provided ideal spaces for the storage of wine. The town's character extends out into the surrounding villages and to the wine châteaux, creating a wine landscape that links together nature, history, and the wine economy of the region.

If our study stopped with the wine, we would miss the wine culture that has developed in Saint-Emilion. The history of the town and its wine have become intertwined. Wine is part of its history, its culture, and the social life of the town. Twice a year (the third Sundays of June and September) the residents celebrate that history in the Jurade. The rest of the year the wine culture of Saint-Emilion is on display in a less formal manner, welcoming wine tourists to the town and its châteaux. Although the landscape and character of Saint-Emilion has earned its recognition by UNESCO as a landscape of historic importance, it is not a museum. It is an ideal place to visit if you want to truly experience a wine landscape.

Chapter 3

THE CLIMATOLOGY OF VITICULTURE

If your favorite local wine shop is anything like mine, they arrange their wine displays in one of two ways. One is by wine type the other is by the country of origin. There may be displays where wines from different regions are grouped together because they are on special or because they are high-end wines locked away for the most serious of gourmets. More typical are rows of California wines (possibly with a few Oregon or Washington state wines mixed in), French wines, Italian wines, and maybe a row containing a smattering of German or Spanish wines. In recent years your wine store has probably given the Australian wines their own row. If your store is big enough there may even be rows that contain wines from places like South Africa, Chile, New Zealand, eastern Europe, and the eastern Mediterranean. Why these places and not Norway, Kenya, and Ecuador? Why is wine produced in so many different parts of the world? The answer is climate. Problems with soils, pests that target grapes, transportation difficulties, economic embargoes, and cultural differences can be overcome. But what we cannot do, except in a greenhouse, is beat climate.

Weather fluctuates from day to day, but over long periods of time, it falls into predictable patterns. Climate is the weather patterns of a place considered at scales of hundreds or thousands of years. Over such spans of time, climate has an impact on plant and animal life, soil development, and influences the character of our culture. As such, it is of profound importance to our understanding of viticulture and wine landscapes, and is a building block of *terroir*.

With any kind of plant-based product, there is a relationship between the plant and the climatic conditions in which it thrives. If we compare maps of world climates, patterns of natural vegetation, and types of agriculture, they will tend to have similar patterns. The plants we grow as food crops today were once part of the natural landscape. Yes, we have tinkered with those plants, in some instances for thousands of years. In doing so, we have changed the plants in remarkable ways, but what we have not been able to do is disconnect them from climate. Corn, for example, evolved through time from tall grass species. If we have a climate that is good for tall grasses, like the eastern Great Plains, then we have one that is good for growing corn.

Climate determines the spatial limits of where wine grapes can be produced. We can manipulate the grape, change its DNA, and create artificial environments where it can flourish, but market economics and considerations of wine quality invariably lead us back to the climatic limits of the grape. To produce grapes for quality winemaking we need a long but not blazingly hot growing season, a winter that is short and not too severe, an adequate amount of spring and early-summer rainfall, dry conditions in the late summer and fall, no late-spring frosts, and no early-fall frosts.

There are a variety of systems used to classify climate. Their general purpose is to make great amounts of data on temperature, precipitation, and seasonal weather variations easier to interpret. One of the most common is the Köppen system. If you have a map of world climates it is probably based on the Köppen system, in which climates are labeled with two- and three-letter combinations beginning with A, B, C, D, or E. Like other systems it considers patterns of temperature and precipitation, and how these fluctuate through the year. It can be used for broad climatic classification or for very detailed and specific climate work.

Those of you who are avid gardeners might have noticed that garden catalogs, plant labels, and seed packets often include information on climate, or maps of plant hardiness. These maps are based on the U.S. Department of Agriculture plant hardiness classification, and their intention is to show where the plant in question will survive. In some ways such maps are of climate. In some ways they aren't. The hardiness measures used are based on low temperature extremes. They are meant to tell us what are the lowest temperature levels that a plant can tolerate. They do not deal with the plant's moisture and precipitation requirements. That is why Phoenix, Arizona, and Orlando, Florida, are in the same hardiness zones. The assumption here is that we can provide for the drainage or irrigation requirements necessary for the plants to grow. Hardiness will tell us where grapevines will survive *if* we can provide for their moisture needs. This might work for some plants. As we shall see later, it does not help us much with grapes.

In agricultural circles the use of plant hardiness is rather limited. More common is the use of growing degree days (GDD). Like hardiness, GDDs consider one aspect of climate, that being temperature. As opposed to hardiness, GDD reflects total heating over the growing season. As such, it is related to the concept of cooling degree days that we use in discussion of energy use for home air-conditioning. What it does is to give us mechanisms for discussing seasonal temperatures and the availability of energy for the processes of photosynthesis and plant respiration.

The calculation of GDD is based on average daily temperatures compared to a benchmark of 50 degrees Fahrenheit. For every degree that the average daily temperature exceeds 50 (65 if you are calculating cooling degree days for your air conditioner), you add the excess degrees to a running total. So for 55 degrees, you would add 5 to your total number of degree days. At the end of the growing season, April through October (grapevine bloom to grape ripening), those numbers are totaled. If you are lucky, wine production is possible below 2,000 GDD. Ideally the range is between 2,500 and 4,000 GDD, the equivalent to a growing season with average temperatures around 75 to 80 degrees Fahrenheit. You can go over 4,000 GDD and still produce meaningful wines. But high heat can severely limit grape production and quality.

Although not foolproof, GDD measurements can be used to draw meaningful comparisons between the growth environments of different wine-producing regions. The idea is that areas with similar GDDs should be able to produce similar wines. Compare Bordeaux, the Finger Lakes of New York, and Coonawarra in Australia. Compare Tuscany, Cape Town, and the Central Valley of California. If we believe the theory, then these regions should be similar based on their climate. The problem is that the theory is very difficult to test. We would have to be able to control for a dozen or so other variables that could influence the quality of their wines, which would be very complex. On a much more positive note, it could be the basis for a lot of wine tastings.

Plant hardiness maps and growing degree days reflect temperature and thus address one part of climate classification. To understand the geography of wine we need more and we get that in the Köppen system. The Köppen system translates a myriad of different climate variables into a set of climate classes. The system takes some of the language that we associate with climate and formally defines the terminology using climate data. This eliminates any ambiguity in the meaning of terms such as "tropical" or "desert." The climate map in the appendix uses the basic Köppen system. So even though we may be familiar with the general use of the terms, a bit of translation is still required for us to use it to talk about wine.

Before we look at climates suitable for wine production we need to get specific about one important point. We are talking about making wine from grapes. This is important because wine-making can make use of almost any fruit. If we include pineapple wine, cranberry wine, plum wine, and all of the other nongrape wines, our map of wine and climate is going to be very different. These grape alternatives allow for winemaking in areas that would not be well suited to grape winemaking. As cultural geographers we can have all sorts of fun looking at how the climatic limitations of wine grapes have led to other wine and nonwine alcohol alternatives. But for now let's just stick with grapes.

The most basic level of classification in the Köppen system breaks down climate by conditions of temperature. This creates broad climate classifications, analogous to how colors are classified. There may be hundreds of shades of blue, and each shade may be important in some way, but all of them are still blue. This is what we are looking at with the most basic designations of climate. No matter how many local variations there are, all climates fall into one of five classes:

Tropical climates where all months average over 64.4 degrees Fahrenheit

Desert climates that have moisture deficits (more evaporation than precipitation)

Subtropical climates with mean monthly temperatures between 26.6 and 64.4 degrees Fahrenheit, where most wine production occurs

Continental climates with one or more months averaging over 50 degrees as well as one or more months averaging below 26.6 degrees Fahrenheit

Polar climates with average monthly temperatures below 50 degrees Fahrenheit

On the climate map we will see that there is a pattern to these broad classifications. As we move from tropical to polar in this system we are also traveling from the equator to the poles. If the earth's surface was uniform (all oceans or all continents)

the pattern would be very regular. But it isn't, so we notice little irregularities in the pattern here and there.

To provide a higher degree of detail, the broad climate classes are subdivided based on precipitation. Some climates have balanced precipitation all year long. Other climates' peak precipitation is concentrated during the summer or winter. This occurs in areas where seasonal weather shifts create a summer or a winter dry season. The desert climates do not have seasonal precipitation designations because, after all, they are deserts. The seasonal rainfall pattern is an important detail as far as wine production is concerned. A balanced pattern of rainfall can be good for grape growing. A summer dry season may be even better. Wet summers create problems for growing grapes and producing wine.

In addition to the pattern of precipitation, we can add to the level of detail by including additional details on peak temperatures. It is useful detail if you are looking at agriculture and, more important for us, viticulture. The key numbers here are 70 and 50 degrees Fahrenheit. Some plants are relatively easy to please. If it is warm enough for photosynthesis (typically 50+ degrees), they are happy. Others are much more finicky. They may need a certain number of warm months (above 70 degrees). Or they may need a certain number of cool months (below 50 degrees) if they are evolved for periods of dormancy. Grapes may not be as demanding as some plants, but they do have specific needs in order to be at their best. They need a warm summer. As they have evolved for winter dormancy, they also need a cool winter. As such, the more detailed climate data is important for determining where viticulture will and will not work.

We associate wine production with a very limited number of climates, specifically ones like those of the Mediterranean basin. Of course, wine can be produced outside these climatic regions. Human ingenuity and sometimes luck make such things possible. But our ability to overcome these problems does not necessarily make wine production economically feasible. Wine can be made from grapes grown in an Antarctic greenhouse, but that doesn't make it anything more than a very expensive hobby.

If we want a climate ideally suited to vegetative productivity it would be the tropical climates, those that are hot all year round because they are at or near the equator. The change of seasons does little to alter the incoming radiation from the sun. The heating in equatorial regions produces massive amounts of convectional rainfall. The air heats up throughout the day, causing it to rise. As it rises it cools, loses its ability to hold moisture, and an afternoon rain shower is the result. This happens on an almost daily basis. The result is a climate characterized by constant warm and wet conditions.

While tropical conditions may be great for some plants, they are not for grapes. You may have noticed in your wine atlas that there are few wine-producing areas anywhere near the equator. It is not that grapes will not grow in a tropical climate. They will. Grapes grown in a tropical environment just won't be good for winemaking. Without a period of dormancy or rest, wine grapes produce poorly for wine. Most plant species adapted to climates with a true winter cool period, need that period to be at their best, and the even, yearlong warmth of the tropics does not provide such a period. As we will discuss at length in chapter 6, wine grapes need a two- or three-month cool period during which temperatures consistently are at or below 50 degrees Fahrenheit. By definition, this does not happen in the tropics.

If we search and search it may be possible to find some isolated locations in the tropics that provide the necessary cool periods for quality wine production. The problem is that although these locations may be in the tropics based on their latitude, they are highland areas that are not tropical in climate. Even if we cheat and include these locations in our discussion of tropical climates, dealing with the heat is only one part of our problem. Part of our definition of tropical climate is based on precipitation. They get a heck of a lot of it. So even if we find locations with the right temperature characteristics, the problem of excess moisture inherent in these climates is very difficult to overcome. This is especially true of monsoon climates that receive massive amounts of rainfall at the exact time of year (late summer) when we want dry conditions for wine grape production.

Desert climates are found in two different circumstances. Most of the world's great deserts are centered around 25 degrees latitude north or south. The rising fountains of hot air at the equator cool as they rise. They then cascade back to earth on either side of the equator. As the air sinks, its temperature rises. This has the effect of drying out the air (rising heat means falling humidity) and creating the desertlike conditions. The deserts of Africa, the Middle East, Central Asia, Australia, and the American Southwest are the result.

The other condition under which we find deserts is as a result of the rain shadow effect. As air is pushed up and over high mountains, it cools and loses its ability to hold moisture. For the windward side of the mountains this means wet weather. When that same air passes over the top and sinks down the other side, it begins to warm. As warming air means drying air, the leeward side of the mountains is drier. It may even be dry enough to be classified as a desert. The deserts on the leeward side of the Himalayan Mountains in Central Asia and the Andes Mountains in South America are prime examples of this effect. Closer to home, the Coast and Cascade ranges in Oregon and Washington produce a rain shadow effect that is profoundly important for their wine industries.

Regardless of how a desert is formed, its arid conditions make growing grapes difficult at best. Deserts are characterized by moisture deficits. They may get rainfall, but the potential for evaporation far exceeds the available moisture. If we can overcome that deficit through irrigation, then grapevines can grow and flourish in these regions. The problem is that irrigation is not the easiest thing to manage. The spray irrigation that many of us use in our yards is not conducive to grape irrigation in desert climates. Spraying loses a lot of water to evaporation as it flies through the air. With grapes we also need to target our watering. Spray irrigation is great for lawns where every inch of grass is important. In a vineyard we don't need to spread water over every square inch of land. We need to focus our watering on key spots. For that we use drip irrigation. Drip irrigation uses perforated hoses either laid on or buried under the surface to put down a steady stream of water at key points. In a desert climate the advantage of drip irrigation is in its ability to target watering and its minimal evaporation losses.

This is not to say that spray irrigation isn't useful. It may be a poor choice for watering desert plants, but it is useful for lowering temperatures and preventing grapes from turning into raisins. As water evaporates it pulls heat out of the air, effectively lowering the temperature. In fact, this is the basis for evaporative or "swamp coolers" that are used as air conditioners in some arid climates.

The first problem with irrigation is access to water, which is not always available in a desert climate. Second, the water must be safe to use. Groundwater and surface water may have natural pollutants that limit their utility for irrigation. Third, the cost of pumping water, especially if it is being pumped a long distance, can be prohibitive, and may make irrigation unaffordable. If these three problems cannot be overcome, then any discussion of drip versus spray irrigation is irrelevant.

Unlike tropical climates, desert climates do have some potential for quality wine production. This does not mean that just any desert can be brought into production. Some deserts are so hot and so dry as to exclude any reasonable attempts at viticulture. But there are places that have the potential to produce quality wine grapes. For example, Elgin, in southern Arizona, has conditions that are more akin to dry grassland (steppe) than a true desert. Here grapes can be grown and wine can be produced. Nevertheless grape-growing conditions are still not ideal and require a fair amount of human intervention to make it work.

For many forms of agriculture, continental climates are ideal. Introductory geography textbooks make connections between continental climates and the production of grains, vegetable crops, and other forms of agricultural produce. They have moderately long growing seasons, hot summers, and plentiful rainfall throughout the growing season. This makes them great for most forms of agriculture. However, this makes them marginal for viticulture and wine production.

Continental climates are produced by an effect called, appropriately enough, continentality. Large landmasses such as continents heat up and cool down much more quickly than the surrounding oceans, resulting in significant seasonal weather variations. In summer they experience warm if not hot weather, low air pressure (due to the heating), and receive the bulk of their annual precipitation. In winter they experience very cold conditions, high air pressure (due to the cooling), and limited amounts of precipitation in the form of snow. The bigger the continent the greater is this effect. In the southern hemisphere we don't see continental climates because there is little landmass outside the tropics. This is in contrast to the northern hemisphere where most of the landmass is outside the tropics. North America, Europe, and Asia are in just the right latitudes to produce continentality. As such, continental climates dominate these landmasses.

Continental climates may be perfect for growing most vegetable and grain crops, which grow quickly in the summer heat and take advantage of the limited growing season. But producing quality wines in a climate best suited for corn or wheat is a complex and risky endeavor. It takes knowledge, skill, and often considerable luck. While in the occasional good years continental environments may produce high-quality wines, there may be many bad years when wine production may be marginal at best.

Many relatives of the wine grape are indigenous to and flourish in these environments. So do many crops that are used to produce other forms of alcohol. Vintners utilizing wine grape varietals can find locations where they can successfully practice their craft. But even in these areas quality wine production can be a real challenge.

Precipitation can be a problem for vintners in continental climates. Continental climates typically have a summer maximum precipitation or a balanced yearly pattern of precipitation. This may be great for your vegetable garden but it is far from ideal for wine production. Late-summer and early-fall rainfall may produce large crops of juicy grapes. Unfortunately they produce weak or "flabby" wines. Late-season moisture also creates an ideal environment for the growth of molds. Some vintners deal with excess soil moisture by planting the spaces between rows with crops meant to remove water from the soil. Proper pruning and spraying may help to alleviate some mold and fungus problems. However, an ill-timed rain near the end of the growing season may turn a great crop into one that is merely okay. With this in mind, wine producers in these areas can often be found poring over weather forecasts so as to time their harvest to precede rain showers.

Another major constraint for wine production in areas of continental climate is temperature and the length of the growing season. As we shall find in discussing the growth patterns of wine grapes, there are certain points of the growth cycle at which temperature is critical. There are also stages of that cycle where grapes are susceptible to extreme cold. What this means is that a late-spring or an early-fall frost may have disastrous results.

There are ways to deal with the problem that may make it possible to produce viable crops in frost-prone areas. Rocky soils absorb and hold heat, and planting on hillsides can concentrate heating. Some vintners spray-irrigate during frosts because, ironically, the ice that forms on the plants can actually insulate them against the colder outside air. Wind machines and propane heaters are also used to fight frost. All of these practices can effectively combat light and infrequent frosts, but they may not be economically feasible in areas prone to heavy and repeated frosts. Also they will not protect the plants in instances where temperatures dip low enough to actually kill the plants.

Grapevines are fairly hardy plants and can survive in a variety of different climates. However, our use of the grapevines requires that they do more than just survive. We need them to survive and flourish so they can produce the quality and quantity of grapes that we desire. While grapevines can be grown in many different marginal climates, large-scale viticulture is still limited to a few ideal wine climates. So what, then, are the ideal climates for wine? We have not discussed the subtropical and polar climates. The polar climates we can dispose of quickly, for obvious reasons. That leaves us with the subtropical climates.

Subtropical climates are usually found nestled in between the desert and continental climates. They present vintners with the right combination of a long growing season, warm temperatures, and a cool winter rest period for high-quality wine. The question in the subtropical climates is precipitation. Subtropical climates with summer peak precipitation dominate most of India and China. These are not prime grape-producing regions as they are simply too wet during the late summer. Some of the subtropical climates with balanced precipitation, like those in the southeastern United States and in parts of Brazil have so much rainfall and are so close to being tropical that they cannot support wine production. And some of the colder subtropical climates found in northern Europe and Alaska are simply too cold for wine grapes. But within the subtropical climate class you do find the climates that we most associate with wine production. They are the Mediterranean and the Marine West Coast subtypes.

Of the classifications present in the Köppen system, the ones most strongly associated with wine production are the Mediterranean climates. They are referred to as Mediterranean climates as they are the dominant climates of the Mediterranean Sea and its surroundings. They are typically found at 30 to 45 degrees latitude (either north or south), and have relatively mild winters and warm dry summers. Although they may experience cold weather, they do not have more than a couple of months when the average temperature is below freezing. They may approach desertlike conditions, but have more moisture than you would find in a true desert. In summer, the combination of heat and low rainfall results in dry conditions that make it difficult for plants to survive unless they are adapted to those summer drought conditions. Plants adapt to these conditions by being summer dormant or by developing thick waxy leaves that help the plant to retain water. Grapes adapt by developing deep root systems that can tap water stored deep underground.

Mediterranean climates are in the transition zone between hot deserts and cooler marine climates farther from the equator. During summer, the arid conditions and high temperatures associated with the deserts move over these regions, rendering these climates desertlike. During the winter, cooler and more humid conditions return. The cool and moist winter conditions are why these regions are not classified as deserts. This climate is a product of the earth's tilted axis of rotation. The 23-degree tilt, relative to its orbit around the sun, is what causes the seasons. And without this tilt there would be no Mediterranean-type climates. That would be tragic as most wine-producing areas of California, Spain, Italy, Australia, South Africa, and southern France are found in areas of Mediterranean climate.

In their suitability for grape growing, Marine West Coast climates run a very close second to Mediterranean climates. They are located next to and poleward of the Mediterranean climates, and are found, as one would expect from their name, on the west coasts of continents. At middle latitudes, the westerly winds coming off the oceans moderate the temperatures of these climates. Farther inland the climate may be continental, but the marine location moderates the conditions enough for them to be classified as a subtropical climate. The key for grape growing is to be in Marine West Coast climates that are as close to the equator as possible. That is because the Marine West Coast climates extend far from the equator, to places such as Scotland, Norway, and Alaska. Although these places may be good for producing other kinds of alcohol (we will discuss Scotland and whisky in a later chapter), I would wager that you probably have not had a great Alaskan wine.

While the Marine West Coast climates can be well suited to grape production, they are distinctly different than the Mediterranean climates. They are cooler and wetter and have less of a summer drought. That said, they are not poleward enough to be too cold or wet enough to be too wet to produce wine grapes. They are different than the Mediterranean climates, though, and support different kinds of vegetation. Vintners in these regions tend to look toward grape varietals that are better adapted to cool weather and do better in wetter conditions. When we compare Oregon with California, Alsace or Burgundy with Provence, or Germany with Italy we are essentially comparing Marine West Coast and Mediterranean climates.

SPAIN

A near-perfect example of a Mediterranean climate is Spain's, with the exception of its northern coast and some of the more mountainous areas. In part this is due to Spain's latitude. It is also a product of the rain shadow effect. The result is not a uniform climate. Rather it is one which, while still being Mediterranean, tends to get hotter and drier as we move from north to south.

As with all Mediterranean climates, Spain's summer weather is very hot and dry. The northern shift of the subtropical high brings hot, dry, sinking air that during the rest of the year is parked over the Sahara Desert. What differentiates Spain from some of the other areas of Mediterranean climate is that the rain shadow effect limits the amount of winter precipitation that the country receives. If Spain were perfectly flat, cooling winds from the north would bring rain and snow from off the North Atlantic. But Spain is not flat. In northwestern Spain the Cordillera Contabrico, a mountain range that roughly parallels the coast, is high enough to produce a rain shadow. Farther east, the Pyrenees are an even more imposing barrier. In combination, these mountains (along with lesser ranges in between) isolate Spain from much of the wet weather that occurs farther north.

The rain shadow effect and the seasonal shift of the subtropical high temperature mean that Spanish vintners have to be adept at dealing with drought. Even though much of central Spain is at elevations over 1,000 feet, the resulting cooling does little to temper the summer droughts. In fact, temperatures in some Spanish wine regions can be hot enough to actually shut down photosynthesis. The obvious response to drought, at least for those of us who measure our self-worth by the quality of our lawns, is to irrigate. As we discussed earlier, this is drip irrigation. However, many areas lack enough water to make irrigation viable. The use of irrigation is also an issue of vineyard economics. The cost of installing, maintaining, and using irrigation systems favors large producers with deeper pockets. That said, irrigation is still of interest to small-scale vintners because it allows for denser plantings of vines and higher levels of production per vine. This can be enough to offset the higher cost of operation and to pay off loans taken out for system installation. But even if vintners have the water, can afford to use it, and are allowed to use it, it may still be too hot and dry to produce grapes for wine production using ordinary vines, and, in fact, vines adapted to colder and wetter conditions are rare in Spain.

Just because it is extremely dry does not mean that we need to immediately turn to irrigation. Simply by increasing the spacing of rows in vineyards, vintners can counter drought conditions. The greater the space between rows, the greater the area over which the vines can draw water. This allows individual plants to better respond to dry conditions. But the downside is that there will be fewer rows and less production. To prevent the loss of water to other plants, vintners in drought-affected regions will do what they can to combat the growth of weeds and grasses between the rows (if indeed such plants will actually grow). These plants are of no economic value, so there is no value in keeping them when they draw water that could be better used by the grapevines. Vintners can use water catchments around the individual plants to try to catch runoff. They can also try various methods to block surface winds that would otherwise increase the rate of evaporation. Browse through pictures of Spanish vineyards or look for it during your next visit. You will undoubtedly see these practices in the Spanish wine landscapes.

In addition to using drought-appropriate planting practices, Spanish vintners are adept at using grape cultivars that are drought adapted. These plants can survive in conditions that are too hot and dry for ordinary cultivars. Some are more bush-like in form. Growing as low-lying bushes they have less exposure to the sun than vines trained high on trellises. In some Spanish vineyards these cultivars don't use any trellises at all. Beyond the form of the plant, some plants are adapted to use less water. They may have smaller leaves or leaves with waxy coatings that slow the loss of moisture.

It may seem strange to follow up a discussion of extreme heat and drought with one of cold-weather problems, but that is the interesting thing about Spain and its climate. The mountains of the north are not a high and solid wall. Weather systems can pass over the coastal mountains. The mountain ranges are also crossed by valleys that act as conduits for the cold, damp air from off the Atlantic. The Pyrenees are a much more significant barrier to cold northern air than are the other mountain ranges. However, in fall and winter cold mountain air can drift down into the valleys. These cold winds can shorten the growing season for wine regions along Spain's northern frontier. As many Spanish wine regions are in plateau country, their elevation will result in cooler temperatures and may influence wine production. The result is that vintners have to deal *both* with heat extremes in the summer and cold problems in the fall and spring.

To cope with the heat, Spanish vintners have traditionally used drought-adapted grape cultivars that are well adapted to the climate. They are well known and loved by the Spanish, although outside Spain they can be a bit of a mystery to wine consumers, mainly because of a lack of name recognition. Names such as Rioja, Navarra, and Castilla-Leon don't mean much to many consumers. Although they are the most important wine regions in Spain, they still do not have the name recognition of Bordeaux, Burgundy, and Tuscany. The problem of name recognition extends also to some of the most common Spanish grapes. Tempranillo and Garnacha Tinta (even if it is written as grenache), are not as familiar to American ears as chardonnay or cabernet sauvignon.

Over time recognition of Spanish wines has improved greatly, thanks in part to their quality. Part of it is also a growing understanding of what Spain is all about. For a long time, the world did not seem to know exactly what to do with Spain, isolated as it was under the Franco regime from the economic mainstream. But that is no longer the case today. Some of the hottest properties in Europe are on Spain's Mediterranean coastline. Spain is home to some of the most recognized teams in professional sports, and is becoming much better known in the wine trade. Whether it is through advertising their native wines or by adopting wine-production techniques and grapes that are more widely known, Spanish wines are showing up in increasing numbers on American shelves.

Chapter 4

MICROCLIMATE AND WINE

When we talk about climate, *terroir*, and wine, we need to deal with issues of scale. Scale is a common geographic concept. We use it on maps to refer to distances and the amount of detail that can be shown. It is a very important concept when we talk about climate. Looking at climate is like looking at a Seurat painting. Seurat was a French Impressionist painter who created his paintings using pinpoints of color. When seen close up they are just colored dots. At a distance those dots form complex images. Climate is like that, too. What at a distance appear to be broad climatic regions break down to a myriad of local climatic variations when we change the scale. We call these localized climatic variations microclimates. It is why the *terroir* of one vineyard can be different from the *terroirs* of its neighbors even if all other natural factors are the same.

Climate is not uniform. To classify climates we use broad ranges of temperature and moisture data drawn from a handful of weather stations. Those ranges, however, allow for a good deal of local variability. The ridge top and the valley; the southern slope and the northern slope; all fall within the same broad climatic classification. Even so, they may still have significant differences in temperature and moisture. For example, we see this in Connecticut, where coastal conditions are always slightly different from those inland. The differences persist through time. They are not temporary aberrations. The result is that there are microclimatic variations within larger climatic regions.

We hinted at these local climatic issues in the preceding chapter when we discussed Marine West Coast climates. Ireland, England, France, and Germany are dominated by such climates. High-quality wine can be produced in these climates if (and it is a big if) we are in just the right places. Germany is Marine West Coast and produces great wines, but it does not produce them everywhere. The great German wines come from specific places where local conditions are suited to the production of wine grapes. It certainly does not hurt to have a little bit of luck with the weather. It also helps to have grape varieties that are adapted to colder conditions, but that is a subject for a later chapter.

So what does it take to make wine in climates that normally are not all that good for grape production? It takes just the right location. If you have a wine atlas or photo essay handy, thumb through to pictures of German vineyards. Most likely, some of the photos will show steep sloped vineyards overlooking a river. After all, some of Germany's best wines come from vineyards in the Mosel Valley and in some of the other valleys that are tributaries of the Rhine River. Perhaps your map shows the areas of wine production in the region. Even better, it may distinguish between areas of average-quality production with those that produce superior wines. Ideally, your wine atlas will have maps that show the shape of the land surface or topography.

For those of you who don't have a wine atlas, or who haven't mastered the art of reading topographic maps, the pattern of wine production is evident mostly on south-facing slopes. Even more, the best production areas are on steep south-facing slopes just above the rivers of the region. And if we want to get really nitpicky, then the very best production areas are on the middle of steep south-facing slopes just above the rivers of the region. The explanation for this is microclimate. But saying that the explanation is microclimate is akin to saying that a car moves because it has an engine. Technically, that is the right answer, but it still does not tell us much.

Local variations in climate can occur due to a variety of reasons. Slope can influence the angle of incoming radiation, soil moisture, wind exposure, and cold-air drainage. Proximity to a body of water can regulate temperature and minimize temperature swings. Elevation can have a profound effect on temperature and precipitation. Even what is on ground level may have a significant impact on temperature. When we start to put these things together, we can end up with a great deal of spatial variation in areas that all have the same broad climatic class. We need to understand these variations if we want to come to grips with climate, *terroir*, and wine.

To understand the impact of land surfaces on temperatures and microclimate, consider the following example. It is a bright sunny August day in Tucson, Arizona. It is 110 degrees Fahrenheit in the shade, we are barefoot, and are trying to walk across town without our feet ending up looking like something that came off of your barbeque. What surfaces would we want to walk on? How about the lawn? Maybe the concrete sidewalk is a good bet. How about the asphalt streets? Would the manhole cover in the middle of the street be a sanctuary for our feet or a griddle?

In general, the temperature will be fairly constant across town. There will, however, be some significant localized variations. Some surfaces reflect a lot of the incoming radiation from the sun. That reflectivity (measured in percent) is called albedo. If a surface reflects incoming radiation, such as the grass and concrete, then little heat will be produced. Other surfaces, such as metal and asphalt, absorb a lot of radiation and thus produce a great deal of heat. The result is that the grass and concrete should be safe for walking while the asphalt and metal will be hot enough to cook meat. We may not notice the difference five feet above the surface, but at the surface our feet definitely will. (Please note that while it may be possible to cook meat on a bare metal surface in Tucson in August, the temperature will never get high enough to kill off all the bacteria in the meat. You've been warned!)

This discussion of surface heating is an extension of the continentality discussion from the preceding chapter. There is, however, another element of the surface heating equation that we need to be concerned with. Go back to our walking barefoot analogy. Change it to nighttime and that we are looking for the warmest surface. Here the issue is not which surface heats up the most. It is which surface retains that heat the longest. Retaining heat becomes an important consideration when our goal is to plant early in the year, grow late into the season, and avoid evening chills and frost. So when we talk about rocky soils in chapter 7, do not think of them as rocks. Think of them as a collection of heating elements.

Another factor that influences temperature is elevation, which is why it can snow at the equator. Temperatures decrease as we get farther away from sea level. In fact, the environmental lapse rate (the rate of that change) is 3.2 degrees Fahrenheit for every thousand feet we go up. There may be instances where there are temperature variations that do not correspond to the environmental lapse rate, but they are just temporary. So when you are flying across country at around 30,000 feet, you are flying through air that is almost 100 degrees cooler than at sea level. Next time you are on a flight where they display the temperature outside the airplane you can check this.

The cause of this temperature change is that the atmosphere is thickest at its base. As we move up through the atmosphere it becomes less dense and the air pressure decreases. That change in density means something as far as temperatures are concerned. It means that there are fewer molecules in the atmosphere to convey heat. It also means that with fewer molecules and lower air pressure less heat is produced through friction as those molecules move against each other. As less heat is produced, less is conveyed by the atmosphere, resulting in cooler conditions than in areas where the atmosphere is thicker. Incidentally, there is also less of an atmosphere to filter out harmful forms of incoming solar radiation, so not only will we get tired more quickly than we do at lower elevations (due to lesser amounts of oxygen), we will sunburn more easily.

What this means for vintners is that where weather is cool we want to be as close as possible to sea level. If conditions are already on the verge of being too cold for wine grapes, we do not want to make things worse by planting at higher elevations. On the flip side, there are locations where it is too hot for wine grapes. To counter the heat, we can look to higher elevations where conditions may be better suited to viticulture. This is how vineyards can flourish in areas that would otherwise be too hot and dry (such as in the Elgin, Arizona, example cited in the preceding chapter).

Even if the elevation is the same, there will be some temperature variations from one side of a hill to another. The side of a mountain facing the incoming rays of the sun is going to receive more concentrated radiation and thus produce more heat. The side of the mountain facing away from the sun is going to get incoming radiation that is less concentrated and will experience lower levels of heating. If the side of the mountain facing away from the sun is in the shade for even part of the day, the incoming radiation will be even less. This is true for mountains. It is true for hills. It is true of even the most gentle of slopes. If you are in a snowy climate, watch the snow melt in the spring and note which side of a hill the snow melts on first.

If we are trying to produce wine in a warm climate, the slope of the land and its effect on temperature may not be a major concern to us. If we are in a climate that is cool, then slope may be a significant concern. Even though the difference in heating may amount to only a few degrees each day, those degrees (remember growing degree days) do add up over the course of a year. Those degrees can also be quite important if we are concerned about the length of the growing season, early and late frosts, or providing growing conditions that are warm enough to produce good harvest. If that is the case, then slope and the direction that the slope faces may be of vital importance for grape production.

The impact of slope on microclimates goes beyond issues of heating. It is also a factor in the relationship that exists between slope and air movement. Locations at the top, middle, and bottom of the same hill may have the same amount of incoming radiation and produce the same amounts of heat, but they will experience differences in temperature and moisture because of effects of cold-air drainage and wind exposure. As such, what grows at the bottom of the hill may not grow at the top. What this means for vintners is that a slope that gets the same amount of incoming solar radiation, and produces the same amount of heating, may not be uniformly useful for producing wines.

During the day, heating of the atmosphere causes hot air near the surface to rise. At night this process reverses as the atmosphere begins to cool. As the air cools it becomes denser and tends to sink. The coldest air will be the densest air and it will sink to the lowest locations. Cold air will "drain" into the valleys—hence the term "cold-air drainage." The valley will be colder at night, more likely to experience frosts, and will heat up more slowly during the day. In climates that are already on the fringe of being too cold for grape production, this may be enough to make grape production impractical in the valleys. If not impractical, it may significantly affect the quality of the resulting wine.

If cold-air drainage makes the bottom of a slope a less than desirable location for grape production, the top of the slope may not be much better. The top of a hill, as you may know from personal experience, is the part most exposed to wind. Windchills will thus be higher at the top of a hill than at the bottom. While we do not normally think of windchills with respect to plants, those winds do have an effect. In addition to the chilling effect, more wind means more potential for evaporation. This too can affect vines and their ability to bear fruit. The effects of cold-air drainage and wind exposure can be mitigated by some cropping practices. Planting rows up and down—not across— the slope, as well as pruning away vegetation near the surface, can make it easier for cold air to flow downhill. These practices are unsuitable for most crops. The resulting soil erosion exposes roots and leaves a very rocky surface. Pruning away foliage is also not practical for crops where the foliage is what is harvested. It is only the deep rooting of grapevines and the harvest of their fruit that makes these practices feasible for vineyards.

What this means is that in cool climates we want to plant on slopes facing the sun. We also want to plant in the middle of the slope. That way we get the benefits of heating and are less exposed to the wind and the effects of cold-air drainage. We will be able to see the difference in the vines and taste it in the wine. This is often illustrated in high-quality wine atlases that include topographic maps.

In the world of real estate, waterfront properties are nice things to have. People like to live near the water both for active recreation and for the enjoyment of the view, and they pay extra for the privilege. In economic terms, the water is an amenity. Water bodies also have an effect on local climatic conditions, and accordingly, waterfront property may be valuable to local vintners as well.

As we discussed earlier, water has a moderating effect on temperatures. It takes water longer to heat up during summer than land does. It also takes that water longer to cool down in winter.

Daily air temperatures may fluctuate a great deal, but water temperatures may not change much at all. Cold air flowing over a warmer body of water will be heated by that water. Hot air flowing over a cold body of water will be cooled by that water. The net effect is that the water we like to live near and look at reduces daily and seasonal temperature fluctuations.

The effect that bodies of water have on the air that flows over them can be important if a vineyard is downwind from a large water body. Even if the water body is not all that big, growing conditions upwind and downwind may be different enough to affect the grape varietals that are grown, and may determine whether we can grow grapes at all. The heating and cooling impact may not be more than a few degrees, but in a marginal climate, a few degrees can be the difference between a good crop and a bad one.

The reality is that the heating and cooling of air moving over a body of water is not that simple. A site that is downwind from a body of water in summer may be upwind from that water body in winter (and vice versa). The impact that the water body has on moisture levels in the air also needs to be considered. The same body of water that provides temperature benefits may also produce moisture problems. And in cool climates, the moderating effect of a body of water in temperature will lessen as it begins to freeze over. So the ultimate rule for water bodies, microclimates, and wine production is that there is no rule. It is just one of those things that we must consider on a site-by-site basis.

All of the microclimatic issues discussed above make any discussion of wine and climate very complex. They also make it almost impossible to find any two places with identical climatic conditions. This may be terribly aggravating if our goal is to talk in generalities about vineyards and climate. On the other hand, it means that every wine could, and should, be a little different and well worth the sampling.

THE RHINE AND ITS TRIBUTARIES

If we want to produce wine in a cool climate, one with a short growing season and early frosts, how would we do it? It is an important question to ask because there are some locations where the link between climate and wine is tenuous. These are locations that would seem to have climates that at best are only marginally acceptable for wine production. However, these same locations can produce consistent yields of great quality wines. The key is to fit production to the environment and get everything we can out of the conditions at our disposal. To do it we also need to find grape varieties that are well adapted to such an environment. The Rhine and its tributaries is such a region. Riesling is the grape.

The climate of the Rhine River basin is not ideal for viticulture and wine production. To produce wine here is to force-fit an agricultural activity into a region for which it is not necessarily well suited. To make it fit requires grape varietals that are cool-weather adapted. In the Rhine basin we have that in the Riesling, Sylvaner, Spätburgunder (pinot noir), and Müller-Thurgau grapes. We also need to find ideal locations within the region. Not just any place will do.

If you have a good wine atlas, this would be a good time to grab it. Browse through the maps of the German wine regions.

If the maps in your atlas include the topography (the shape of the surface) you will begin to notice a pattern of vineyards located on south-facing slopes above major rivers. Not all wine-producing regions in Germany will follow this pattern exactly, but many of the best ones do.

The reasons are fairly simple. The southern exposure of these slopes maximizes the heating effect of the sun's rays. The slope also allows cold air to drain into the valleys. Vines are pruned and planted to facilitate the cold-air drainage. Although this produces erosion, that erosion creates a rocky soil surface that heats up nicely during the day and holds that heat better at night. The woodlands at the top of the hills protect the slopeside vineyards from the cold winter winds. In some instances even the reflection of light off of the rivers can factor into the microclimates of the vineyards. In other words, hundreds of years of practice and experimentation have produced a wine region that is a fantastic example of how to make use of microclimates. Riesling grapes are well suited to this environment because they tolerate cold weather better than other grapes. Because they mature late in the year, they can take advantage of the last few warm days of the fall. Rieslings do not produce large volumes of wine per acre, so they are typically found only where cold weather precludes other grape varietals.

The hillside vineyards are not only the place to see microclimates at work and to taste great Rieslings. They are also the places to see traditional viticulture. The steep hillside locations are poorly suited to most forms of mechanized agriculture. In fact, machines may be limited to the lifts that carry the harvested grapes down into the valley. This helps to explain why most wineries are in valleys. It has always been easier to take the grapes down a hill than to hoist them up. The steep slopes of vineyards place a premium on human labor. As the cost of labor in Germany is not insignificant, wines from hillside vineyards (in Germany or anywhere else that has high labor costs) will probably be higher. However, if you like great Rieslings, the cost will be worth it.

For geographers, the interest in Rhine basin wines goes well beyond the topic of microclimates. Over time the Rhine and its tributaries such as the Mosel have cut deep valleys. As the rivers meander back and forth (the S-shaped bends in the river), they have widened the valleys. On the outer edges of the meanders the water speeds up and erodes the walls of the valley. On the inner edges of the meanders the water slows, depositing debris carried in the river and forming a floodplain. The deep valleys and winding rivers constitute the natural landscape on which has developed the fascinating cultural landscape. On the south-facing slopes there are vineyards which make use of every advantage that the microclimates of the valleys have to offer. The north-facing slopes are typically forested since other crops that are suited to the climate are not suited to hillside locations. Exposed hilltops along the rivers are dotted with castles. The strategic value of such locations is recognizable even today, especially when you walk up from the valley floor to visit them. The rivers are flanked by roads and railroads that take full advantage of the flat terrain of the floodplains. (Trains are especially poor at dealing with hills.) And wherever the floodplain is wide enough we find other crops more traditional to cold climates. If cold air drains into the valleys, the floodplain crops either tolerate it or are harvested before it becomes a problem.

What we also find in the valleys are towns and villages, some of great age and history. They developed in the valleys because there they could take advantage of the agricultural lands of the floodplains and the transportation routes afforded by the rivers. If we take a closer look at these valley towns, we will find that many of them are nestled in the small bits of floodplain on the insides of the river bends. These locations are protected from the erosion of the river that takes place on the outside edges of the meanders. In the event of flooding, these villages are situated outside the floodways, which means that, although they would be inundated, they would not be subject to the power of rapidly flowing floodwaters. The age of the settlements and the wealth of the river valleys mean that the riverside villages have some of the best examples of traditional architecture.

The valleys of the Rhine and its tributaries are great wine places. As landscapes, the mix of picturesque villages, winding rivers, and hillside vineyards creates some spectacular scenery, where the interplay between climate and wine is at its most vivid. From hilltop to hillside to valley, you can see where climate and wine work together and where they don't. More important, the region produces some spectacular wines. This makes them ideal places for visitors interested in soaking up the regional character, eating some great food, and drinking the best wines that microclimates can produce.

Chapter 5

Grapes, Soil, and _Terroir_

Soil is a pivotal consideration in the production of wine. The physical and chemical properties of soil affect the health of grapevines and the properties of the grapes they produce. There are those who claim to be able to taste soil differences in various wines. Admittedly I have never been one of those people. But that does not necessarily mean anything since I have already admitted to drinking generic beer. To those who can taste the difference, the beauty of soil reaches right into the bottle. So never refer to soil dismissively as dirt. It is literally the foundation of quality winemaking and the basis of *terroir*.

If you are a gardener, you probably know good soil when you see it. Even people who have never planted a seed have some basic notion of what good soil looks like. Or at least they think that they do. That is because, as is often the case in life, looks can be *very* deceiving. Soil that is great for vegetable gardening may be useless for any plant that roots deeper than the length of a shovel blade. Likewise, soil whose surface resembles a gravel driveway may be a great resource once we get past the surface layer of stones. Grapevines can easily root to depths exceeding five feet. So in the case of wine and soil, we must remember what our parents told us: Beauty is more than skin-deep.

SOIL BASICS

Assume for a moment that we are all basically ignorant about the joys of soil. It is all just dirt to us. However, what we want is to be able to discuss wine and soil in an authoritative manner. To do so, it is very helpful to have some soil to look at, touch, and even smell. Even as novices we can learn many things about soil simply by direct observation. It might not make us one with the earth, but at least getting our hands dirty will give us some "feel" for the material.

Soil has texture. If we rub it between our fingers we will feel gritty bits that are actually grains of sand, one of the inorganic components of the soil. The soil may smell, usually from gasses held in it or from decomposed organic matter. Soil may feel moist due to accumulated water. In other words, based on our direct observations of the soil we are able to deduce some of that soil's basic properties and components. It may not be splitting the atom, but it is not bad for simply playing in the dirt.

If we want to build on our observations, a good place to start is with the inorganic components of soil. These come to us through the weathering of rock. Through weathering, rock is broken down into smaller and smaller particles that are capable of supporting plant life. Those particles can be moved around by water and wind, becoming incorporated into the soil. Weathering can be a physical process (sometimes referred to as mechanical weathering), where rock is literally broken apart, or it can occur through chemical processes.

Chemical weathering requires at least a passing appreciation for chemistry. If we can understand how acids dissolve materials or explain what happens when metals rust, then we can come to grips with chemical weathering. Picture those processes occurring in rock, but just picture them occurring very slowly, all the time, and at a pace that is visible only at a microscopic level. In the weathering of soil, chemical nutrients are released into the soil and into water trapped in it. Over long periods of time, this weathering maintains the supply of chemical nutrients and ensures the ongoing productivity of the soil. Without weathering, plants and the movement of water through the soil could remove nutrients, lessening its productivity.

To understand the impact of soil's inorganic components, think about a large piece of rock. That rock may contain many of the same chemical compounds that we would find in fertilizer. The problem is that as a solid rock, those compounds are impossible for plants to get to. Weathered into small, sometimes microscopic pieces, those compounds are accessible to plants. They fertilize the soil. They make the soil a better medium for the growth of grapevines. As such, they influence the ability of those plants to bear fruit and affect the chemical qualities of the fruit. Therefore, weathering becomes important to the production of wine.

In addition to inorganic materials, organic components to soil include products of the decomposition of organic matter (leaves, plant roots, and so on)—what is called humus. Humus benefits the soil in ways that are different from but complementary to the weathered materials. To understand how decomposition introduces organic matter into the soil, consider a mulching lawn mower. The lawn mower cuts grass into countless tiny pieces that are left behind in the lawn. Where do all those pieces go? In a warm, wet environment, like my lawn in summer, those pieces decay and become humus. Over time that humus becomes part of the soil. This can happen in many ways. Even children playing in the grass can help the humus to become incorporated into the soil. The important thing is that the humus adds greatly to the productivity of the soil. Through time its benefits carry downward into soil layers well beneath the surface. This is important because, unlike grasses which root a few inches deep, grapes can root down deep into the soil. Even so, they benefit from the creation of humus near the surface.

The organic materials that are worked into the soil are very important to the things that live in it. Those little bits of grass contain nutrients that the grass pulled out of the ground as part of its growth cycle. The fertilizers that we spread on our lawns are also in those bits of cut grass. So putting the grass back into the soil in the form of humus puts the nutrients back into the soil. As an additional benefit, the decomposed organic materials are good at holding on to moisture. Think of all those little bits of decomposed grass as tiny sponges. The net effect is that organic materials mixed into the soil provide plants with nutrients and hold the moisture that they need to survive.

As we dig down through the soil the ratio of organic and inorganic components changes. At the surface, soil tends to be high in organics. There are even soils which have surface layers, or "horizons," that are almost entirely organic. This makes sense because decomposed organic materials are being introduced into the soil at the surface. Likewise, new inorganic materials are being produced deep in the soil as bedrock slowly weathers. As we move down through the soil horizons the proportion of organic materials decreases while the inorganic ratio increases. In a young soil this transition may occur over only a few inches. As this process continues over long time periods (thousands of years), the depth of the soil will increase. What was once the thinnest of soil may become many feet of soil with the passage of time.

This variation of soil with depth is advantageous for deep-rooting species such as grapes. Each horizon of soil may have something different to offer the plant. Some horizons might be good for certain kinds of nutrients. Others may be good for catching and storing water. In these horizons the grapevine may grow extensive root systems to access everything the soil has to offer. Other horizons may have little to offer the plant. The vine will root through these layers to seek out more productive horizons below.

Climate is very important in the production of soil, and in weathering. In cold climates repeated seasonal freezes can produce high rates of physical weathering. Freezing and thawing of water in the rock can break it into pieces. This is true for rock and for the rocklike materials (such as concrete) that we use for pavement. Pavements will crack over time with continued use. Water caught in the cracks freezes and expands, cracking the pavement further. This process is repeated until the broken pavement gets swept away by snow plows. Plant roots, especially those of trees, wedging their way into the rock can have a similar effect. If there are mature trees in your neighborhood then you can probably find a place where their roots are buckling the sidewalks. Obviously if the climate does not support repeated freezing or the growth of trees then such physical weathering will be limited.

Climate's impact extends also to chemical weathering in that temperature affects the speed of chemical reactions. Chemical reactions, including the decomposition of organics, occur faster at higher temperatures. In hot climates, as in the tropics, chemical weathering and decomposition will be more rapid. In cold climates, that same amount of weathering or decomposition may take much longer. If you want proof of this, take some of those grass clippings that we discussed earlier. Put some in the freezer, some in the refrigerator, and some on your bathroom counter. In short order you will see the impact of temperature on chemical weathering. And whether it is chemical or physical in nature, the rate of weathering will have an impact on the ability of grapevines and other plants to find the nutrients they need in the soil.

The impact of climate on soil formation and on vegetation is such that maps of climate, soil, and surface vegetation will have very similar patterns. This is a very useful learning tool. On the surface we can see vegetation; the same cannot be said for climate and soil. But if we know how vegetation, soil, and climate relate, we can infer what we cannot see. We can compare maps, see the commonalities in the pattern, and begin to work on the reasons why the commonalities exist. Consider the following two examples.

Oxisols are soils that dominate in rain-forest climates. A tropical rain forest is made up of tall broadleaf evergreen trees growing in ideal conditions of warmth and moisture. Such warmth and moisture rapidly decomposes organic materials and produces high rates of chemical weathering. Unfortunately the water in rain forests tends to wash the organics and nutrients right out of the soil. The result is that oxisols are heavily weathered with little in the way of nutrients or organic content. Nutrients are present, but they are all in the trees. This means that not only are tropical climates poor for growing grapes, because of temperature and precipitation problems, they are limited because their soils have few of the nutrients needed by the vines.

Aridisols are desert soils. A desert environment has cacti and other plant types adapted to hot and dry conditions. The dry conditions mean that there is little surface vegetation and limited amounts of organic content in the soil. The absence of vegetation means lots of erosion. With dry conditions there will also be limited chemical weathering; rocks will weather more slowly and be exposed at the surface by erosion. As a result, aridisols will often have a rocky surface with little in the way of surface organics. When weathering does occur there is little moisture to wash the nutrients out of the soil. For grapes and other plants this can be a good thing. If vintners can overcome the problems of extreme heat and lack of moisture, the nutrients trapped in the soil can make aridisols useful for grape production.

Soils form slowly over very long time periods. How they form depends on more than just climate. Soil formation is influenced by climate as well as by bedrock geology, vegetation, topography, and the passage of time. If we know what to look for, soil is a good recorder of what the environment has been like over the centuries. Has the site been swampy or dry? Have conditions been warm or cold? Was the site forested or covered by sand dunes? All of these things and more may be reflected in the soil of a given location.

In navigating the basics of soil we can cover a lot of ground (so to speak) before we have to get into the geographic material. At some point, though, we have to deal with the fact that soil can be fully understood only in relation to its geographic context. That is because we cannot really understand soil without appreciating the importance of place. Geology, vegetation, topography, and climate vary from one location to another. So do the soils they produce.

Topography is the form or shape of the surface. Depending on the location, it can be the most important factor in soil formation. That is because topography is a primary control of soil erosion, transportation, and deposition. If the entire world was flat and windless, these processes would have no affect on soil. Obviously that is not the case. As we discussed in the preceding chapter, hillsides are often very desirable locations for vineyards. Consequently we need to know how topography affects the soils of those vineyards.

Erosion is simply the removal of material through the movement of wind, water, or ice over a surface. As vineyards and glaciers are seldom found together, we can ignore ice as an erosional force. Water and wind erode materials and transport them to other locations where they are deposited. When we look at vineyard soils, we need to consider the impacts of erosion and deposition as both affect soil quality and productivity.

Consider erosion and our grass-cutting example from earlier in the chapter. The dust and debris kicked up by the lawn mower is a product of erosion. The lawn mower blows it into the air. The resulting clouds of dust may seem rather insignificant until we consider the slow pace of soil formation. Each cloud of dust could represent a year or two of new soil development. Consider, however, not only the amount of dust, but what is *in* it. Those clouds of dust may be very high in organic matter and plant nutrients. That is what makes up much of the surface soil of a lawn. As the dust blows away what is lost is some of the soil's productivity. The soil lost through erosion does not merely disappear. It has to go somewhere. It may travel a few feet or hundreds of miles. When it is deposited someone else will benefit from the organic matter and the plant nutrients that you have lost.

The importance of erosion is that even at slow rates, erosion can exceed soil formation. Erosion of the soil surface has the effect of removing organic materials while leaving behind the inorganic components. Where erosion is high, even these materials can be removed, leaving behind exposed bedrock. Depending on the rate at which it occurs, erosion can thus impoverish the soil of nutrients or remove it completely.

When it comes to presents, it is better to give than to receive. When it comes to the movement of soil through erosion, the opposite is true. The deposition of material by wind or by water can introduce organics and plant nutrients that were eroded from other locations. In limited amounts this is a very good thing. Deposition is a sort of natural fertilization of the soil. Over time, agricultural societies located on the floodplains of rivers have counted on seasonal floods to provide that fertilization.

In those societies, floods are not seen as a hardship but as part of the cycle of life. In some cases, the use of dams to prevent flooding and/or to produce hydropower have disrupted these cycles. The classic example is the Aswan Dam on the Nile River. The dam generates a huge amount of electricity for the people of Egypt. It has also prevented the floods that occurred each year, and in doing so has forced Egyptian farmers to use fertilizers to make up for the loss of deposited nutrients that used to come with the floods.

Deposition becomes a problem when there is too much of it. Taken to extremes, existing soils may be completely buried by the deposited materials (called alluvium). Although even a moderate thickness of alluvium can cause short-term problems for the established root systems of plants, in the long term, deposition can play a starring role in soil development. That is because soil deposition can take place at speeds that far exceed soil formation through weathering. A single flood may deposit more soil than could be formed in a lifetime. We refer to soils created by repeated deposition as alluvial soils. Where these soils exist, weathering may be of only marginal importance.

Alluvial soils are fairly easy to recognize. It is simply a matter of looking at the soil horizons (layers). In a soil that has developed in place, the horizons will be related. The characteristics of one will transition into the next and the next and the next. In alluvial soils, the horizons often bear no relation to one another. They are like layers in a cake. They will be different in color, texture, and "flavor."

The best indicator that a soil is alluvial is that it will have horizons of uniformly sized particles. This is because wind and water sort materials as they transport them. Water moving quickly and in large amounts has great power. If the water slows, or if there is less water, then there is also less power. Water that could carry away your car at high speeds may be able to carry only gravel-sized particles at moderate speeds and clay-sized particles at very slow speeds. A horizon of sands and gravels may represent deposition by fast-moving water. The very fine layers above and below that horizon may represent deposition by slow-moving water. Wind does the exact same thing. It just does not do it as well as water. The resulting layers in the soil may persist indefinitely. Over time, they can become permanent as layers in sedimentary rocks.

The particles that make up the soil are not trivial. When soil scientists use terms like gravel, sand, silt, or clay they are referring to the size of soil particles (in descending order). The exact ratios of these materials that are present in the soil are the basis for how we classify their soil texture. To do this we make use of a little tool called a texture triangle. By using the triangle to graph the percent of sand, silt, and clay, we can classify its texture. Gravel and other particles larger than sand are not considered part of the soil's texture, according to the USDA classification system. A loam is not a loose or ambiguous term for a soil; it is an example of a texture class. In this case, it is a class that has relatively equal amounts of sand, silt, and clay. As we shall see below, the importance of soil texture for grapes and other plants lies in its impact on the ability of the soil to hold water.

The reason soil texture is important is that it influences the infiltration rate, percolation rate, and porosity of the soil. Translated into plain English, this means that the texture of a soil affects the rate at which water enters the soil, the rate at which water moves through the soil, and the amount of pore space in the soil. If we take a bucket of water and pour half of it into a child's sandbox and the other half onto bare soil nearby, we will see the impact of soil texture. The rule here is that the smaller the particle sizes (the more clay), the longer it will take water to move into and through the soil. In fact, some clay can have particles that are so small and tightly packed together that they do not permit water to flow through. Before landfills started using plastics to prevent leachate (water that has pulled chemical elements out of the landfill deposits) from entering the soil, responsible landfill owners lined the base of their landfills with thick layers of clay. The clay layer would slow or stop the flow of leachate into the soil below. Clay is still used as a base for new landfills even if it is only to support and reinforce the plastic liners.

Soil texture is also very important in determining the ability of the soil to retain water. If we turn over a shovel full of damp soil, some of the moisture may escape. Then again, it may not. The water that remains in the soil does so because the tension that exists between the soil particles and the water molecules is enough to keep the water in place. That tension influences the value of the soil for agriculture. We want a soil that is able to hold water, but what we do not want is so much tension that plants are unable to draw the moisture out. The level of tension is based on the texture of the soil.

We classify water held in the soil using the terms hygroscopic, gravitational, and capillary water. Hygroscopic water is the term used when the tension is so great that plants cannot pull the water out. It is there, but the plants cannot get at it. The only way to extract this water from the soil is to evaporate it by baking the soil at high temperatures. Obviously that is not very useful for agricultural purposes. The opposite of hygroscopic is gravitational water, where the tension is so minimal that water actually flows through the soil. If we turned over a shovel full of damp soil and water did flow out, that water would be gravitational water. Gravitational water may be of limited use in farming as it simply flows away after each rainfall event. In between hygroscopic and gravitational water is capillary water. This is water held in the soil at a tension level greater than that of gravitational water but less than that of hygroscopic water. It is this level of tension that is important for plants.

A side view of a grapevine's root systems will illustrate the importance of soil horizons and their ability to hold water. Soil horizons that are high in sand will not hold much water. Capillary water flows through and out of these layers. As such, sandy soil horizons are a virtual desert for the plant. Its roots will simply grow through such layers in the search for nutrients and water. Layers of soil that are high in clay may hold water, but it is hygroscopic, and will be held at such high levels of tension that the plant will not be able to make use of it. As in a landfill, a layer of clay may be so impervious to water that it actually traps water above it. This may soak the above-lying soils to such an extent that the soil becomes a poor medium for most plants. This will be evident in a limited amount of rooting. The best soil combination is one in which there is a mixture of clays, sands, and silts. There needs to be sufficient clay, especially in summer-dry climates, to slow the passage of moisture and retain it. At the same time there needs to be enough silt and sand to allow for moisture to be held as capillary water and to prevent soaking.

From sand to silt to clay, the tension levels that hold moisture in the soil increase. This obviously has an impact on the ability of plants to access the moisture held in the soil. Moreover, it influences the ability of plants to access nutrients in the water. Consider this the next time you are confronted with a bag of fertilizer. Assuming that the fertilizer is free of pesticides, weed killers, and fungicides, the bag will include instructions for watering. Some fertilizers are even applied in liquid form. The reason is that many of the nutrients that plants draw from the soil are water soluble. That makes the soil's ability to hold moisture extremely important.

When we look at soil as a basis for plant growth, we should think of it as a grocery store. Soil contains all sorts of chemical compounds that are used by plants, some of them vital to the plant's survival. Others serve more specific functions, such as to support plant reproduction, root growth, and fruit development. We pick up a gallon of milk from the corner store. A plant draws potassium from the surrounding soil.

At a very basic level, plant nutrients come in two types: Cations are positively charged particles, which include potassium, calcium, magnesium and iron, and anions, negatively charged particles, which include phosphorus and sulfur. If there is a bag of fertilizer in your garage its ingredient list will likely include many of the nutrients from this list. Whether the nutrients come from fertilizer or directly from the soil, grapevines pull them in along with the water absorbed by the plant roots.

Some soils are better sources of these nutrients than others. Clays and humus have very high cation exchange capacities (CECs). In other words, they are very good sources of plant nutrients. Sands tend to have very low CECs. Silts are somewhere in the middle. What this does is to add another layer, so to speak, to our consideration of soils for grapevines and wine production. Not only do we need to look at the pattern of plant rooting for access to water, we must examine the pattern as it applies to nutrients. The roots are accessing not only water but cations for their use in the production of chlorophyll and foliage, or anions for their use in plant development. For grapes, we can see the influence of the soil in more than just the root system of the plants. We can also taste it in the resulting wines.

After all this discussion, can we finally talk about what makes for a good soil? The answer is no. That is because there is no single definition of a good soil. A soil that is great for one use may be poor for another. So defining a good soil requires that we specify how it is to be used. We can make a few generalities in defining a good soil, the most basic of which is that soil should not "do" anything to excess. This means that

- Clay is good in moderation because it provides nutrients and helps to slow water as it drains through the soil. Too much clay is bad because it can limit root penetration and trap water, resulting in flooding and waterlogging. Clays also hold water so tightly that plants may not be able to extract the water from the soil.

- Sand is good when mixed with silt and clay to create loamy soils. Too much sand creates a soil that is incapable of holding any moisture and is a poor medium for plant growth.

• Water in the soil is necessary for plant growth. Too much water and most nonwetlands plants will die. Too little water and plants will wilt and die.

• Plant nutrients are necessary for healthy plant development. Too much of any one of those nutrients can have the exact opposite effect.

In general, soils that are good for agriculture are those that are deep, well drained, loams to loamy. Loams are composed of roughly equal parts of sand, silt, and clay. Such soils should have decomposed organics and have recently weathered inorganic materials. There are certain types of plants that may be able to thrive in less than ideal conditions. Some soil conditions can also be "helped" by human intervention.

VINEYARDS AND SOIL

The link between soils and agriculture is readily seen in the concept of *terroir*. In theory, *terroir* includes the consideration of soils, geology, weather, climate, topography, and culture. In application, *terroir* is based heavily on soil. An online search using the term "terroir" will produce photos of crops, foods, and a lot of pictures of soil. This is because soil is very specific to a place. Of the environmental components, it is the most variable. It also has a direct impact on the health and productivity of plants, including grapevines. The qualities of the soil can have an impact on what crops will grow. The qualities of the soil can further influence the produce from those crops. Wine lovers can literally taste its influence.

Consider the example of the Mosel Valley from the preceding chapter. The picture that we have of the valley is of steep south-facing hillside vineyards. We talked about the hillsides and microclimates. What we did not consider in that discussion was the soil component of that picture. Hillside vineyards tend to have rocky surface soils. In some cases this may be a natural feature of the soil. In most cases it is going to be a factor of erosion. The rocks are present on the surface because all of the lighter particles have been washed away. Normally farmers try to limit erosion, especially if they are dealing with shallow-rooting plant species. They do this by planting across the slope. In doing so, each row of plants serves as an impediment to erosion. The deep-rooting grape makes this less of a concern. The rocky surface covering may limit some of the erosion. More important, the heating characteristics of those rocks may be a real advantage in cool environments where frost is a problem.

Anywhere that we find vineyards planted on hillsides we need to consider the soil and the bedrock geology of the site. This is especially true if the geology varies across the site. If the entire hill has the same geology, then the weathering of the rock underneath will produce the same nutrient mixture over the entire slope. On the other hand, if the slope cuts through layers of rock that are different, then the nutrient mix that is produced through weathering will vary. Erosion will transport materials down the slope, influencing the fertility of the hillside below. This can have a significant influence on the productivity of grapevines and may even result in the use of different grape varietals on the upper and lower sections of a hillside.

In the case of the vineyards on alluvial soils, it is important to remember that the soil horizons may be variable in character. Even if the surface soil is quite poor, there may be very good soils deeper down. This is where a deep-rooting plant like a grapevine has an advantage over shallow-rooting crops. Grapes can compensate for infertile soil horizons and horrible surface soils by pushing roots down to nutrient- or moisture-rich soil layers. This advantage allows viticulture to take place in soil environments that would be impractical for other forms of agriculture.

As a case in point, try the following the next time you are online. Go to your favorite search engine and do a search on "Lanzarote" and "wine." Lanzarote is part of the Canary Islands chain, located off the coast of Africa. The islands are of volcanic origin, which will be readily apparent when you see pictures of them. The vineyards there are unlike any others. Most crops will not grow there because volcanic ash is exceptionally poor at holding water. However, grapevines can survive because of their ability to project roots deep into the soil, where the soil is better able to hold moisture. The result is an odd-looking landscape of black volcanic ash with thousands of pits where the vines have been planted. The pits help to collect the very limited amount of rainwater. Enterprising vintners have even erected small walls to protect the vines from the winds that would increase evaporation from the plants. The result is a landscape of low-lying, crescent-shaped volcanic rock walls, each with a pit and a vine inside. It has a very otherworldly look about it.

The link between soil, grapes, and wine is profound. Soil is one of—if not *the*—primary environmental factor in *terroir*. As a result, soil is celebrated and revered by vintners. Places such as Lanzarote provide some extreme examples of the link between soil and wine. We do not need to venture that far afield. We need go only as far as our local vineyard to see the impact soil has on grapes and wine.

BORDEAUX

One of the best places in the world to look at soil, *terroir*, and wine is Bordeaux. The city and region of Bordeaux are all about wine and wine culture. The region is known for its high-end red wines, typically cabernet sauvignons, and impressive wine châteaux. This reputation could give the false impression that Bordeaux is only about wealthy wine châteaux and cabernet sauvignon. The truth is just the opposite. Bordeaux is a diverse wine-producing region, thanks in large part to the soils of the region. As such, it is a great place to look at soils and their influence on wine.

A soil map of Bordeaux will be quite complex and, at first glance, may be difficult to understand. With a little background information, however, we can begin to make sense of the map. We have already discussed alluvial soils. If we add a little bit of information about rivers, glaciers, and their impact on soils, we can start to understand Bordeaux's complex soil environment and the wines that it produces.

Most of the wine production in Bordeaux comes from the alluvial soils of the Gironde River and its tributaries, the

Garonne and Dordogne. The rivers have played an important role in the development of the region's soils. Today they meander gently through broad floodplains, carrying modest amounts of water from the Pyrenees and the Massif Central, slowly depositing sands, silts, and clays as they flow through Bordeaux. Thankfully this has not always been the case. If we turn back the clock to the last ice ages, we find a much different situation. The rivers are fast flowing and wild, carrying huge amounts of glacial outwash. It is this history of the rivers that is the basis for the most productive wine *terroir* of Bordeaux.

During the last ice age, the Pyrenees and Massif Central were heavily glaciated. Those glaciers contained, in addition to large amounts of ice and snow, materials that had been eroded as the glaciers moved. With warmer temperatures, either due to elevation differences or climate change, the glaciers melted and released large amounts of water. That water carried with it the eroded materials from the glacier and anything else it picked up along the way. As a lot of water was flowing quickly down from the mountains, it had the power to carry a lot of material.

Pictures of glaciers, especially those that terminate on land, typically depict a winding pattern of small streams at the base of the glacier. These braided streams are a product of the deposition of materials carried from the glacier. The water flowing from the glaciers deposits so much material that the stream channels are constantly filling with material and shifting their course. Near the glacier these deposits can contain rocks and gravel. As the water flows farther away from the glaciers, lighter materials are deposited. The water will be light gray in color because of the presence of large amounts of rock pulverized by the glacier. To understand the geology and soils of Bordeaux, picture those braided streams. During the last ice age, Bordeaux would have been covered with deposits of gravels, and sands intermixed with pulverized rock. It is those glacial deposits that are the basis for some of the greatest of the Bordeaux *terroir*. They influence the quality of the soil in terms of its texture and the release of nutrients as the deposits weather, and are integral to understanding the soil map and *terroir* of Bordeaux.

The history of deposition by the rivers contributes to the diverse soil environment in Bordeaux. The slow-flowing rivers of today deposit clay and silt-rich sediments. These sediments are not ideal for grape growing. The better soils, where vineyards are located, are on the older river deposits. They are parallel to, but a respectable distance from, the rivers. There are also areas outside the floodplain, as in the Saint-Emilion example discussed earlier, where the soils are a product of weathering and not of deposition.

Soil diversity is not the only influence on Bordeaux *terroir*. Climate also plays a significant role. Close to the coastline, climatic conditions are maritime. The waters of the Atlantic have a cooling effect during the hot weather of summer. In the spring and fall they limit the daily variations in temperature that can produce late-spring and early-fall frosts. Although the influence of the ocean is positive, coastline vineyards can be problematic. Very thick sand deposits near the coast dramatically limit the availability of water for plants, even those with deep root systems. Salt spray and salt water intrusion into the groundwater supply can also be a problem in coastal areas.

The conditions near the coast make the glacial soils ideal for the production of cabernet sauvignon. The red wines of Médoc, Saint-Julien, Pauillac, Margaux, or Graves are cabernets produced thanks to the qualities of soil and climate in those areas. There may be some merlot or cabernet franc mixed in, but cabernet sauvignon is the main player. The reason cabernet sauvignon is so much a part of wine production in Bordeaux is that this region is one of the few places in France that is ideally suited to the grape. Cabernet sauvignon needs a long growing season and is very susceptible to frost damage. Also it does not produce well in hot weather. As such, the maritime influence (which moderates temperatures and lengthens the growing season) provides exactly what the plants need to produce at their best. Elsewhere in France the limited length of the growing season rules out cabernet sauvignon for all but the Mediterranean environments south of the Alps and the Massif Central. This does not mean that other vines would not produce in Bordeaux. They could. But the economics of cabernet sauvignon is such that if it can be grown, then it is.

Even within Bordeaux, conditions inland can be too continental for cabernet sauvignon. Technically no place in Bordeaux is truly continental, but conditions do become more variable and the growing season shorter as we get closer to the foothills of the Massif Central. With these changes, merlot becomes a much better grape for use by local vintners. As a result we see a transition in Bordeaux from cabernet sauvignon along the coast to merlot in the hills of the interior. There will be many other grape varietals grown in Bordeaux, although their production is limited in comparison.

The soils and climate of Bordeaux are such that the story of the region is really a tale of two wines. There is the cabernet sauvignon for which Bordeaux is famous. It is produced at the great coastal wine châteaux whose names are very familiar to wine lovers. It is the wine that I stare at longingly but can never afford to buy at my local wine shop. Then there is the merlot. It is produced from smaller, less well-known inland châteaux where the influence of the rivers and the ocean are less pronounced. The merlots do not have the name recognition or the price of their more famous neighbors. In both instances they reflect the connections between soils, climate, and fine wines that are characteristic of Bordeaux.

Chapter 6

BIOGEOGRAPHY AND THE GRAPE

There is a tremendous amount of diversity in the world of wine, due mostly to the different grapes that produce wine. If we think of wine as a process and not simply as a product of certain kinds of grapes, then we do not even need grapes at all. The cranberry wines of southeastern Massachusetts and the pineapple wines of Hawaii are good examples of this. If wine can be produced from any sort of berry or fruit, then the possibilities for producing wine are almost endless. The truth is that where producing wine is concerned, not all fruits and berries are equal. Even within the grape (*Vitis*) family the grape varietals identified on wine bottles are not the same varietals listed on a can of grape juice concentrate or on a store display of table grapes. To use an analogy, think about singing. Almost any fruit or berry can be used to produce wine just as almost any person can produce a song. Unfortunately, not everyone can produce a harmonious song.

The most common and well-represented wine grapes are varietals of *Vitis vinifera*. If we stick with our singing analogy, then the vinifera varietals are like great opera singers. Each is recognizable and distinctive. Each is capable of producing tremendous acts of artistry and we come to expect that artistry from them. However, they can produce truly memorable performances only when conditions are perfect. Put the Three Tenors in a high school gymnasium, at an outdoor venue in bad weather, or in a room full of screaming children and you are not going to get the performance that you desire. It may come close, but it won't be perfect. The same can be said for wine grapes. As consumers, we have very specific demands of our wine grapes. We want great acts of artistry from them regardless of the venue that produced them. If conditions are perfect then something truly memorable can be produced. If conditions are less than perfect, we may be looking at the wine equivalent of Pavarotti singing in a broom closet. It may be Pavarotti but the experience will be nowhere near optimal.

What are the perfect conditions for growing wine grapes? To answer that question we need to know about the conditions under which wine grapes evolved. Our best guess is that *Vitis vinifera* originated in the area south of the Caucasus Mountains. The Caucasus form part of Russia's southern border between the Black and Caspian seas. Today that region is a political hot spot. Due to unrest in Chechnya, political instability in Georgia, and the ongoing tensions that exist between Armenia and Azerbaijan, it is a place that few people travel to. Putting the political issues aside, it is a region with warm and relatively dry summers. Winter conditions are cool but not cold as the mountains block the worst of the winter winds. The Black and Caspian seas further moderate temperatures in the region. The forests in the mountains give way to grasslands and deserts in the warm valleys and lowlands. In this respect it is similar to areas in Northern California and parts of south-western Europe.

The importance of this point of origin for *Vitis vinifera* is that it was under these conditions that the grape evolved. Admittedly, humans have done a lot of "fiddling" with *Vitis vinifera* over the ages to allow the grape to thrive in areas that are climatically different than its point of origin. There are also nonvinifera varieties such as the Concord grape that grow in conditions markedly different than the southern Caucasus. Most of the grapes used for wine production are vinifera varietals. To produce wine using the vinifera varietals one requires a climate that is similar to that of the southern Caucasus. Any climate that is markedly different means trouble.

PHOTOSYNTHESIS AND PLANT RESPIRATION

We can associate the geographies of plants to the conditions under which they evolved. To understand the way that plants relate to their environment, we need to observe the way that they work. This requires a passing knowledge of plant physiology, but not enough that anyone should run in fear. We need to know a bit about photosynthesis and about plant respiration. It also does not hurt to understand a little about how the physical form of a plant may be adapted to its environment. This is true for *Vitis vinifera* as it is for corn, wheat, apples, or any other plant used as a food source. The key point is that photosynthesis, plant respiration, and plant morphology link plants to their environment. When we understand these things at even a rudimentary level, we make the connections between plants, climates, and places. In other words, we can understand biogeography.

Photosynthesis is the process by which plants absorb energy and convert it into plant nutrients and is an important process in understanding the geography of plants. Photosynthesis occurs as carbon dioxide, water, and light produce oxygen and sugars for storage and eventual use by the plant. Chlorophyll is instrumental in this process as it turns the leaves into light receptors for use in this reaction. The green coloration of the leaves is a product of the chlorophyll. The stored sugars are used up in the respiration process where they are combined with oxygen to produce carbon dioxide, water, and energy. The production of mature fruit—or, for our purposes, grapes—is tied to the processes of photosynthesis and plant respiration. For geographers, the importance of these processes is that they are dependent on climate conditions: light, moisture, and temperature.

We already know that climate can vary a great deal from place to place, and these variations will impact photosynthesis. Ideally, the leaves of the plant are producing energy at near their maximum capacity. Under less than ideal conditions, those same leaves may end up using more energy than they produce. In very high light and heat conditions the leaves may be unable to keep pace with the available energy. What exactly these conditions are varies from one type of plant to another. On a bright sunny day light levels may top out at about 10 to 12,000 foot-candles (my apologies to those of you who are metric system users). Most plants will not be able to use all that light; they become light saturated at somewhere between 3 to 5,000 foot-candles. Likewise, most leaves become parasitic and use more energy than they produce—somewhere between 150 to 200 foot-candles. The more time that plants are exposed to light at or above saturation levels the more photosynthesis will take place. Plants regularly exposed to low light levels will undergo less photosynthesis. Photosynthesis also responds to heat; the closer to 80 degrees Fahrenheit the better. Depending on the plant type, the optimum temperature for photosynthesis ranges between the high 70s and low 80s in degrees Fahrenheit. At temperatures above or below this range, photosynthesis decreases. Depending on the type of plant, photosynthesis ceases somewhere over 100 degrees and below 50.

We can expand on the link between photosynthesis and climate by including plant respiration. Plants produce sugars from light through photosynthesis. They use up those sugars through plant respiration. In the process they use light energy and water. What this means is that not only are the processes sensitive to light and temperature, they are sensitive to conditions of temperature and moisture. If we assemble the climate-related considerations of photosynthesis and plant respiration, we can conclude that the ideal growing environment has long sunny days with temperatures around 80 degrees Fahrenheit and a steady supply of moisture. In other words, the ideal growing environment in terms of photosynthesis, plant respiration, and the production of biomass is a tropical rain forest. This does not, however, indicate that it is ideal for all plant species and especially not for grapes.

Environmental considerations affect more than only photosynthesis and plant respiration. They also influence the form, or morphology of plants. In a tropical rain forest or in a green-house, we can find ideal temperature, light, and moisture condi-tions for plants. In such ideal conditions plants can support huge leaves that stay with the plant all year long. They are broadleaf evergreens. Most of the world does not have ideal growing conditions. There are locations where the temperatures are too hot, too cold, too dark, or too dry to be ideal. Plants have evolved over time to adapt to less than ideal growing con-ditions. The interesting thing is that many of the adaptations are common to a climate. If an adaptation is good for one rain forest it should be good for others. If an adaptation is good for one hot desert, it should be good for others. This is convergent evolution. Wherever similar climates are located, for instance a Mediterranean climate, we find similar adaptations in the plant species present. As a result, maps of climate and vegetation tend to have much in common.

The range of plant adaptations to their environments is stag-gering. Thanks to convergent evolution we see some of these adaptations repeated in locations around the globe. The species and locations may be different, but the adaptations are the same. This is just as true of grapes as it is for other species. If the environment provides a niche for grape-type species, you will find them there. The grapes may have different qualities in their use for wine production, but they will still look and taste like grapes.

At the most basic level, all grapes are broadleaf deciduous. The term "deciduous" means that they lose their leaves and become dormant during times of environmental stress. For grapes this is due to cold, although there are other species that are deciduous in response to drought. As a survival strategy, being deciduous allows plants to "rest" through periods when their leaves would be a detriment to the plant. They can then grow new leaves in the spring, or when conditions improve. This is an advantage in climates with variable seasonal weather conditions, and a disadvantage in climates that are always warm or where the growing season is too short for the plants to completely replace their foliage every year.

Grapes also have leaves that are big and broad (hence the name "broadleaf"). The advantage to broad leaves is that they provide a large leaf area, which means there is a lot of potential for photosynthesis. It also means that a tall broadleaf tree can shade out its low-lying competition. The benefit of having broad leaves is significant. That is why broadleaf plants can outcompete needle-leaf evergreen trees in most environments. Broad leaves are not, however, good in extremely cold or extremely arid climates.

Together, being broadleaf and deciduous means that grapes are not ideal for tropical climates, extremely arid environments, and extremely cold environments. This eliminates the tropics, most of the desert, cold continental areas, and all of the polar climates.

Grapes are also part of an extended family of fruit-bearing vines. They have seasonal forms: leaves, tendrils, flowers, and fruit. They also have woody features that persist from season to season: the shoots, arms, trunk, and root system. In form, grapes are little different from other vine species. They compete for sunlight by climbing. They compete for moisture and nutrients by rooting deep into the soil. These adaptations are in addition to those typical of all broadleaf deciduous species. This is the "game plan" that allows grapes to survive and thrive in certain climates. The primary difference between grapes and other vines is the use we make of them and the changes that we have bred into them.

The root systems of plants are designed to take in nutrients and moisture for the purpose of supporting photosynthesis, respiration, reproduction, and growth. The pattern of rooting, the plant's method for accessing moisture and nutrients, varies a good deal based on the species and environment. For the *Vitis* family the plan is to set deep root systems capable of accessing moisture and nutrients well below the surface. This is an especially popular adaptation to dry environments where a plant may have to root down a long distance before finding moisture, say, to a depth of six feet or more. There is, however, a good deal of variation in rooting depth. As most woody plant species don't do well when their roots are constantly saturated, rooting depths might be less if water levels in the soil are high. Very heavy clay layers in the soil, or shallow soils where bedrock is near the surface may also limit the depth of root penetration. In coarse soils that are very sandy or that have lots of gravel grapes may root far deeper to access water. Of course, this is also dependent on the age of the plant. It takes time, energy, and resources to develop a root system, especially one that is deep and well developed. As such, older vines will tend to have deeper root systems. The benefit here is that the depth of rooting means that these older vines will be better able to survive periods of drought and to access nutrients deep below the soil surface.

It is important to remember that what we are seeking in a grapevine is only one part of the plant's reproductive process. In some plants we might want big leaves. In others we might want maximum seed production. In grapes we are looking for fruit with just the right properties for the production of great wine. Grapes propagate sexually via pollination and fruiting. For the plants, the purpose of the fruit is to provide an ideal environment for early seed development. It is this part of the plant's life-cycle that humans have most sought to manipulate. As with most other fruit and vegetable crops (wheat, corn, beans, apples, and so forth), we have found that subtle or not so subtle manipulation of the seeding process results in a product that is as good for us as it is for the plant. We manipulate the size, number, and other qualities of the fruit to suit our needs. We have also manipulated the plant's development over time to stretch the range of environments in which they will prosper and to help them ward off disease or pests. These efforts have changed the plant over time. They have not drastically changed the geography of the grape.

THE GRAPE LIFE CYCLE

The connection between plants and their environment is not simply a matter of whether the plants will survive in a given location. It is a matter of whether the plants will be able to reproduce in that location as well. Can the plant live out its life cycle in that environment? Does the timing of when the plant sprouts, sets leaves, flowers, seeds, and so forth, fit the location? I can plant just about anything in my yard. That does not mean that it will survive and flourish there.

The *Vitis* family needs a period of dormancy. A couple of months of cool temperatures, at least in the 40s and 50s, are required to produce that dormancy. What they do not need are extremely cold conditions or an extremely long period of dormancy. While frosts can damage the leaves, shoots, and stems of a grapevine, temperatures near zero can damage even the woody parts of the plant. Damage due to extremely low temperatures can be extensive enough to actually kill the plant. Vintners adapt to possible cold damage by allowing multiple stems to grow. If one should be severely damaged by cold or frost it can be trimmed away, allowing the others to remain in production. Other than during months of dormancy, photosynthesis and plant respiration dictate that the rest of the year be sunny with temperatures around 80 degrees.

Assuming that the plant has survived the winter months, we will begin to see budding and bud break when the average daily temperatures exceed 50 degrees Fahrenheit. Ideally, peak conditions for photosynthesis will be achieved within a few weeks of bud break. By that time the leaves of the plant are fully open and ready to do their work. Depending on the weather specifics, blooming occurs about a month and a half or two months after bud break. During this period the plant is susceptible to late frosts, which can damage emerging leaves and flowers. During bloom the plant is also susceptible to damage from heavy rains and hail. Even without them, it is natural for some of the blooms to shatter and fall from the plant without producing fruit. Shatter reduces the overall number of grapes in each bunch, easing the maturation process for the remaining grapes. Damaging weather can increase the shatter to the point where bunch sizes are significantly reduced.

Blooms that do not shatter will produce fruit. The resulting form and size of the bunch will vary among types of grapes, but the process of development is the same.

The first immature berries set a week or so after the blooms shatter. From that point forward the grapes will mature, slowly losing their green color. Sugars in the grapes increase and acid levels decrease. This increase in sugars will eventually play a role in the fermentation process. Until then, the sugars make the grapes a target for insect pests, disease, and birds, and the susceptibility of grapes to these problems increases as they ripen. High humidity can be especially problematic because it contributes to fungus problems in ripe and overripe grapes. Grapes can also be lost to shattering late in the ripening process. If conditions are exceedingly hot and dry the ripening grapes can dry and turn into raisins.

We need to be careful when talking about the dates for the various stages of the yearly grape life cycle because the dates will vary by grape varietal. Weather preferences will also vary by varietal. That is actually a very good thing. It demonstrates why some varietals work better than others in a given location, and is the basis for the geography of grape varietals.

The life cycle of the grape is what links it to the Mediterranean and Marine West Coast climate classes. The plant needs a period of dormancy followed by long warm growing seasons, both of which are consistent with those climates. The plants need spring and early-summer rains for the initial foliage and grape development, and require long periods of ripening to develop the qualities that make for good wine production. These are consistent with the Mediterranean and Marine West

Coast climates. Moreover, the cool winter temperatures within these climate classes are not so cold as to cause frost damage or plant loss. These make the Mediterranean and Marine West Coast climates productive for winemaking and eliminate the other climate classes for this purpose. They take us back to the assumptions made in chapter 3 and give us our current world map of wine production.

If we were to take that map and look at wine production in more detail, we would find that there are geographic patterns for the individual grape varietals. We would find that as conditions get warmer there would be a transition of the red varietals from pinot noir, to merlot, to cabernet sauvignon, and finally to Shiraz/Syrah. In the white varietals that transition would be from Sylvaner, to Riesling, to chardonnay, to sauvignon blanc, and to pinot grigio. This pattern is not an absolute. Even if the environment was exactly the same, there could be societal preferences and marketability issues that favor certain types of grapes. There are also less well-known varietals that may be very important in specific wine-producing regions. This is part of the puzzle of wine and its geography. The fun is in figuring it out.

THE LOIRE VALLEY

Terroir goes way beyond the environment of a place. *Terroir* is inextricably tied to regional variations in the production of agricultural goods. As no two natural landscapes are exactly the same, there will always be some variations in the products of local agriculture and in the foods and wines associated with that agriculture. Over time these local variations become the focus of regional cuisines, and part of the culture of a place, so what may start as a minor difference in the natural environment becomes much more—part of the cultural identity of a people. It is what distinguishes one place from another and gives variety to the regional cuisines of France. It becomes part of who they are.

The Loire Valley of northwestern France is as good a place as any to study *terroir* and the biogeography of grapes. It is a region of significant environmental contrasts. At its headwaters, the Loire River and its tributaries are located in the foothills of the Massif Central, in an environment that is on the northern fringe of the Mediterranean climate zone. As we travel downriver the valley broadens into a wide plain with deep, rich, alluvial soils. This trip takes us closer to the Atlantic Ocean and into a region of Marine West Coast climate. It also takes us into the agricultural heartland of France. Thanks to a history of châteaux building in the valley and its proximity to Paris, the trip downriver takes us into one of France's most popular tourist destinations.

The problem with writing about *terroir* in any place as large and diverse as the Loire Valley is how to limit the discussion. An entire book can be written on just this very subject. So, rather than covering every *terroir* of the Loire Valley, I will set my sights on three. We will start upstream in Sancerre before moving downstream to the Touraine and then to Nantes. I selected these three for very personal reasons. Come hell or high water Sancerre was going to end up somewhere in this book. I like the place and, more important, I like the wine. So it was an easy choice. Touraine is included for the benefit of those of you who might like to eventually try a wine tour by bicycle. The area has a nice assortment of wineries and a variety of historical sites. It is also flat, which makes for easy sightseeing. Last, I include Nantes because it is a place that links a wine with a regional cuisine, which makes it a good choice for our discussion.

Sancerre is in hill country near the headwaters of the Loire River. It is a pretty countryside of hilltop towns and beautiful views. Unlike some wine-producing regions, Sancerre is not a grape monoculture. It is a productive region of mixed farming. Pictures of Sancerre are just as likely to include cows, sheep, soybeans, and grain crops as they are grapes. Vineyards face the sun on the many south-facing hillsides. In the valleys below, the river has deposited rich alluvial soils of the kind that are great for just about anything other than grapes. In the hills, however, the weathered limestone bedrock provides a real resource for grapes. Rainwater running off the hillside vineyards helps to dry out the soil and render it better suited to grape production. As Sancerre lies inland and at higher elevation than areas downstream, it experiences cooler weather and conditions that are more continental than locations downriver. This diversity in the landscape makes Sancerre a good spot to look at biogeography and the links between plants, microclimates, soils, and topography. It is why I like the place.

The diversity in Sancerre's environment means that many different kinds of grapes could be grown there. Pinot noirs and other wines may be produced in Sancerre, but the ideal grape for the environment of Sancerre is the sauvignon blanc. The grape originated in this region and is thus well adapted to the local conditions of climate and soil. Sancerre is just upstream of the Briare Canal, which connects the Loire to the Seine—and the wine shops of Paris. Given that connection, most of Sancerre's wines have traditionally been consumed locally. They do export their wine, but not in huge quantities. As a result, your local wine store may not even stock them. If you are a fan of sauvignon blanc, the region's predominant wine export, it is worth the effort and the added expense to give their wine a try.

Downstream from Sancerre, in Touraine, we find a very different grape-growing environment. Most people who visit the Loire Valley end up in, or pass through, Touraine because this is where many of the most visited châteaux are located. For our discussion of biogeography the Touraine vineyards are worth looking at because they are linked to the rivers. This is very different from Sancerre, where the vineyards were in the nearby hills. Vineyards in Touraine are located on the slopes paralleling the Loire and its tributaries. Away from the rivers the deep soils are ideal for wheat, sunflowers, livestock, and vegetable farming. In the river floodplains the silt and clay-rich alluvial soils are often too wet for viticulture. But on the slopes overlooking the floodplain layers of limestone rock exposed by erosion fertilize the vineyard soils. The Touraine vineyards are about five hundred feet lower than those in Sancerre and are only around seventy miles away from the Atlantic. Along with the geologic differences, these factors give Touraine a *terroir* that is distinct from that of Sancerre. The result is that wine production in Touraine is based on chenin blanc, gamay, and cabernet franc. Part of the reason for this is that the climate and soil are well suited to these grapes, as opposed to sauvignon blanc. The other reason is cultural.

These are the grapes that have been traditionally grown in the region. Even though other grapes can be produced in the region, traditions of wine production are very hard to change—especially so when they have become part of the culture and identity of a region.

As we travel down the Loire River one of the last stops before the river reaches the Atlantic Ocean is the port city of Nantes. Nantes has an interesting history as far as wine is concerned. As the closest port with significant access to wineries, Nantes was a marketplace for exports to England and Holland. More important, accessing the markets for wine elsewhere in France required transporting the wines upstream over long distances. This raised costs, making the sale of wines overseas a better bet for the wineries of Nantes.

Its proximity to the Atlantic means that Nantes has a distinctly maritime climate. Nantes is not very far from Touraine and Sancerre, but its grape-growing environment is very different. Geologically the area around Nantes is an old coastal plain bisected by a number of small rivers. Producing wine virtually within sight of the Atlantic means that the climate of Nantes is governed by the ocean, which moderates temperatures and lengthens the growing season.

The physical setting of Nantes is not all that different from Bordeaux to the south. One might thus assume that Nantes, like Bordeaux, would be a prime location for the production of cabernet sauvignon. The reality is anything but that. What would seem like trivial differences to us may be very significant to plants. While climatically and geologically Nantes may be similar to its neighbors, the differences are such that it has a distinctly different *terroir*, one well suited to the Melon de Bourgogne grapes used to make muscadet, a fruity white wine that dominates production in the region. The wine *terroirs* around Nantes will often have the word "muscadet" in their names, illustrating the link between the grapes and their *terroirs*.

Nantes, Touraine, and Sancerre are but a few of the wine-producing regions within the Loire River valley. Thanks to variations in the climate, topography, and soils within the valley from its headwaters in the Massif Central to its outlet on the Atlantic, the Loire is a great place to look at the links between *terroirs* and the grapes that they produce. We can literally taste these links in the wines of the valley.

VITICULTURE, AGRICULTURE, AND NATURAL HAZARDS

In learning about viticulture we are actually learning about agriculture and vice versa. It might be difficult to imagine that, while walking through a well-tended vineyard, we are learning a thing or two about growing soybeans, for instance, but that is indeed the case.

For those of us who are incapable of growing anything more demanding than an artificial Christmas tree, do not be concerned. In looking at geography and its links to both agriculture and viticulture, you will not be expected to plant anything. Rather, we look at the interaction of climate, soil, economics, cultural practices and preferences, as well as a good deal of history in order to understand the patterns of agriculture. The point of all this is not to make anyone a farmer. What understanding agriculture will do is to help explain why your favorite wines come from certain regions. A knowledge of climate and soils provides us with part of the answer, and agriculture helps with the rest.

THE GEOGRAPHY OF AGRICULTURE

To understand geography and viticulture, or agriculture, we need to start in northern Germany. That may seem odd as it is not an area known for viticulture. It is there, however, that the modern study of agricultural geography originated in the mid-1800s. Its originator was Johann von Thunen and he was not studying wine. Rather, he was puzzling over the fact that land of the same physical quality was used for different agricultural purposes. It was a simple beginning, but his work forms the basis of agricultural geography to this day.

What von Thunen discovered through his work was that the use of agricultural land varied. Near the marketplace, agriculture was intensive. With proximity to the marketplace, transportation costs to the market would be limited, so nearby land was highly desirable and, therefore, expensive. To make up for the increased costs, farmers would produce as much high-value crop per acre as they possibly could. They used the land intensively, emphasizing highly perishable crops such as lettuce, tomatoes, and peppers. If a crop can spoil in a hurry, then we do not want to be very far from the market.

Farther from the marketplace the land was used less intensively, growing crops that, while important, produced less income per acre. Crops that were easy to transport long distances, such as wheat, barley, and oats, would be common in farmlands at a distance from the marketplace. More valuable crops would be less likely to be found in these areas because the additional transportation costs would make them more expensive than those of competitors whose farms were closer to the marketplace.

The basic assumption behind von Thunen's work was that agriculture was a profit-making venture. This is the "economic man assumption" that is common in the social sciences. It is the assumption that people act in an economically rational manner and have all the information that they need to make sound economic decisions. This assumption may or may not hold true for viticulture. There are many who see wine production as a profit-making venture. There are those who view it as a "fun" profit-making venture. There are also those who regard it as a hobby. Unless your local vintner has very deep pockets and is producing wine purely as a hobby, then there is going to be some economic rationality at work. So even if there is a bit of "fun" involved, there will also be a good deal of von Thunen social science that would apply.

The result of von Thunen's work was the understanding that there was and is a very strong relationship between geography and agriculture. That relationship has three components. First, locations have differing conditions of climate, soil, and topography. This will have an impact on what can be produced in a given location. Second, land costs, transportation costs, and the market value of the product will influence what can be produced profitably in that location. Third, culture and history will determine what people have the knowledge and facilities to produce. In a sense, von Thunen sets forth a process of elimination. Take every single food item that exists. Eliminate those that cannot be produced in a given location. Then eliminate those items that cannot be profitably produced in that location. Then get rid of any food item that people do not have the knowledge or the facilities to produce. What we have left is the range of crop choices that local farmers have to work with. In an economically rational world, the farmers will choose the crop on that list that produces the greatest profit.

Von Thunen's work leads us to the following questions: Based on the environment, where can we produce wine grapes?

Considering land and transportation costs, will wine production be profitable, and are wine grapes the most profitable potential crop? Do farmers have the knowledge, experience, and equipment necessary to produce wine? We can see the results of this line of questioning on wine maps. For every wine-producing area shown on the map, each of the answers to the above questions were yes.

How food is produced and who produces it varies from society to society. There are societies where food production is in the form of subsistence agriculture. Almost everyone is employed producing food and they are producing it for their own consumption. Successful farmers may produce food surpluses that they can trade. Many types of crops are produced through subsistence agriculture, but no wine at your local store is produced that way.

Winemaking occurs at the point where subsistence agriculture gives way to commercial agriculture. Commercial agriculture is food production designed for barter or sale. In commercial agriculture we produce single crops or associated crops. We specialize in those crops, invest in machinery and facilities for their production, and sell them on the open market. The specialization that is common within commercial agriculture can lead to a monoculture. In subsistence farming, we would not find hundreds of square miles of farmland completely devoted to growing corn unless folks *really* liked to eat nothing but corn. In commercial agriculture, however, we find just that. It is commercial agriculture that we are referring to when we talk about von Thunen's work.

While we pay our respects to von Thunen and the agricultural geography of the mid-1800s, it is important to note that there are a lot of new wrinkles to consider. During von Thunen's lifetime the cost of labor varied little from one agricultural region to another. The mechanization of agriculture, which has transformed the industry beyond recognition, was only just beginning. Today we are capable of transporting crops much faster and more cheaply than in von Thunen's day. We can also transport far more food and can preserve it so that it better survives the transport. Together, these have changed agriculture and altered its geography. What this means is that a world map of wine regions from von Thunen's time would have looked very different from the map we see today. This evolution has seen commercial agriculture grow from small family farms to full-blown industrial enterprises. Farm labor is no longer dominated by family groups. Research-and-development departments make recommendations to management on crop decisions. Lawyers are the spokespersons for farming conglomerates that are recognizable only by their corporate logos. Although this change is most pronounced in the world's wealthy countries, it is a trend that is visible in the developing world as well.

The advantage of a more industrialized form of production is in specialization and in resource use. Family farms can specialize, but major corporations can specialize to an extent with which most family farms cannot compete. Corporations have greater financial resources to devote to the purchase of the most advanced agricultural machinery. Those financial resources also allow them to hire the best minds in the business. By sharing those resources among many farms, the corporate producer can make more efficient use of those resources. This gives them a distinct advantage over individual farmers. Even though individual farmers may join cooperatives as a means of contending with the industrialization of agriculture, and these cooperatives can be an effective competitive strategy, they have not proven to be the savior of the family farm.

The economic basis of the new commercial agriculture is the production of high volumes of food with limited labor. This means that societies with industrialized agriculture have few farmers. The people who are not farming are employed in manufacturing activities or in the information and service economy. Such activities produce more value from the same amount of human labor. We call this "value added." The value added by manufacturing eclipses that of agriculture. The value added by information and service activities is beyond that of even manufacturing. As a result, we see a transition over time from agriculture to manufacturing to service and information economies. In the United States, this transition means that very few people are involved in food production. Economically, this is advantageous. Industrialized agriculture does not need a large workforce. It also means that those who do still call themselves farmers treat it as a business.

Another change in modern agriculture that von Thunen could probably not have envisioned is the degree to which government is involved in farming. At the national level, government is concerned about agriculture as a profit-making venture and to support the farm industry. The government may also use agriculture as a means of securing food production for its citizens. This is a common practice in countries that are net food importers. Food production is not, however, why governments involve themselves in viticulture. Government intervenes in viticulture to protect local economies. As viticulture and wine-making can be significant to the cultures of many people, government regulation and oversight may also be seen as a means of protecting the national heritage and of the way of life of its people.

Local governments may also exert a significant influence over agriculture. Many countries allocate land-use controls and property taxation to local government. This gives local authorities a significant amount of power. Also it creates a rather complex political environment of overlapping jurisdictions where the decision making at one level may run contrary to the decision making at another. Each of those decisions could have a significant impact on what crops we are allowed to grow, how we grow them, and which ones are the most profitable. In other words, government affects the answers to the questions that von Thunen was asking. As such, government involvement is a very important "wild card" in the geography of agriculture.

In viticulture and wine, government interference can be quite extensive. For a case study, take a look at the European Union. In the EU political issues concerning wine have reached dizzying heights, whereby considerations such as how wine regions are identified become matters of international importance. This political interest in wine is typically an outgrowth of economic or cultural issues. Individual countries may be members of a unified Europe, but each still has its own individual interests at heart. If you are interested in agricultural regulations, I would suggest reading the EU regulations on wine and viticulture. I would also suggest a very strong cup of coffee.

If we understand the basics of geography and its link to agriculture, then we can move on to the details of its links to viticulture. What kind of agriculture is viticulture? Viticulture involves a crop that is very sensitive to conditions of weather and climate, and that perishes quickly. Grapes have always been rather difficult to produce and transport and thus viticulture is a form of agriculture that has historically had a limited geographic distribution. That said, the growth form allows viticulture to be practiced in areas not suited to other forms of agriculture. It is a form of commercial agriculture that produces a high-value crop that becomes even more valuable with processing, and that benefits from specialization. Viticulture has very high fixed costs requiring a long-term investment strategy. Labor is important for viticulture both in the field and with skilled craftsmen in wine production and support activities. Like most forms of agriculture, profits from viticulture will vary from season to season with the quality of the crop. The strong link between viticulture and environment leads to it being associated with specific places and cultures. This gives viticulture a status that other agricultural activities do not have. Wine production as an element of culture gives viticulture governmental protections.

While there are advantages to viticulture, there are also some very significant disadvantages. Wine has to be a high-value product because the production costs are considerable, partly due to the high cost of labor. Although labor costs can be reduced through mechanization, there are some places and types of production (think back to those Mosel Valley vineyards) where mechanization is just not practical. Even where mechanization is possible, there is still a lot of labor involved. There is no getting around the fact that viticulture is labor intensive and expensive, a situation made worse because the world's wine-producing nations are at the top of the list when it comes to average labor costs.

The recognized link between place and product creates another interesting issue for viticulture. I hesitate to label it as a problem because it is only a problem to some vintners; for others it is an advantage. The tie to culture can create a good deal of chauvinism. We typically do not care where our corn, beans, or tomatoes come from. All that really matters is that they are fresh. The same cannot be said for grapes and wine. For wine, place really matters. This means that good vintners in marginal or little-known wine regions are working at a disadvantage. At the same time, marginal vintners from well-known wine regions operate at an advantage based solely on name recognition.

In our discussion of grapes, wine, and agriculture we need to keep in mind that wine is not the only product that comes from grapes. Viticulture can just as easily produce table grapes and grape juice. In the spirit of von Thunen we need to ask ourselves: Why go through all the trouble to produce wine when it would be much easier to sell table grapes or juice?

In this respect, viticulture is like other forms of agriculture in that determining what to grow or raise is only part of the process. Do we raise cattle for milk, butter, cheese, or beef? Do we grow corn for food or for livestock feed? Do we grow grapes for wine, juice, or to eat? We can answer these questions by going back to von Thunen. First, what can we produce in our environment? If that does not provide the answer, then the question becomes: What choices will yield a profit? If that does not provide the answer, then what do we have the equipment and knowledge necessary to produce? After all, the same cows that are great milk producers are not necessarily good as steaks. Dairying requires very different equipment from ranching or running a feedlot. The labor involved is quite different as well.

Now, if the answers are the same for all of our alternatives, how would we decide whether to produce table grapes, grape juice, or wine? If all else is equal, the decision comes down to which product will produce the best return on our investment. Producing all three requires the same amount of work to get a vineyard into operation. Of the three, wine will have the highest costs postharvest. So why produce wine? Wine will be the highest cost option. It will also provide the highest revenues. When we consider all factors, wine will tend to be our best investment. If we compare the juice it takes to produce a gallon of wine versus a gallon of grape juice, the amounts are similar. However, the gallon of wine will provide significantly greater revenues. Likewise, if we compare the sale value of bunch grapes versus the value of the wine that can be produced from those grapes, the wine revenues will tend to be higher.

Maybe the better question is: Why would we *not* produce wine? Part of the answer is economics. There is a market out there for juice and table grapes. If there is money to be made then somebody out there is going to produce juice and table grapes. There is also a geographic answer to this question. Table grapes and grape juice can and are produced from varietals that are different from those used in winemaking. In some cases those grape varietals can flourish in areas where wine-grape varietals would be problematic. There may also be a cultural answer to why one would choose to produce juice or table grapes instead of wine. We will save that for a later chapter.

An additional use for grapes is in the production of ethanol. Grape production for ethanol is admittedly far from ideal. Any starch or sugar can be used to produce ethanol so why waste good grapes? It is also better from a profit perspective to produce wine or juice or table grapes. Still, if we cannot sell grapes for anything else then ethanol is an option. Taking good grapes and reducing them down to a fuel for our cars is not, however, the most romantic of options.

Just as there is a lot of geography behind how wine is produced, there is also a lot of geography behind how the grapes for that wine are grown, managed, and harvested. For someone who is very knowledgeable about vineyards, a picture of a vineyard may be enough to clue them in on its location. That is because patterns of planting, how vines are trained and pruned, as well as the materials and machinery that are used will vary from place to place. In fact, some viticulture practices are as strongly associated with places as the wines that they produce. So a picture of vines trained high on lines between poles or trees may be enough to identify the location as a Portuguese vineyard.

In countries with high labor costs, mechanization is used wherever and whenever possible. Yes, the tractor and other equipment may be terribly expensive. However, if we consider the amount and cost of labor that they replace then the sticker shock is much less severe. The use of machinery will dictate pruning practices, trellising, planting, and the overall appearance of a vineyard. In a mechanized vineyard we plant with the wheel base of a tractor in mind. We trellis and prune vines with machinery in mind. Anything else would be counterproductive.

The good thing about mechanization is that it helps to keep down costs. The bad thing is that it does away with some of the local flavor of viticulture. Manufacturers make equipment to common standards. Anything else would put them at a disadvantage in the marketplace. Every vintner who uses the machinery will therefore be working with the same planting, pruning, and trellising requirements. As such, mechanized vineyards may all look the same. The only way we can recognize from a photograph where a vineyard is located is from the buildings in the background. However, because an amazing number of wineries end up looking like French châteaux or Spanish haciendas regardless of where they are, sometimes that does not even help.

Mechanization does not work everywhere. There are vineyards on steep hillsides where machinery is simply not practical. There are also places where labor costs are low enough that mechanization is not necessary or profitable. As geographers and lovers of wine, that is a good thing. In these areas we can still see the influence of history and culture on the practice of viticulture. The truth is that many different planting, trellising, and vine-management systems can produce quality grapes. What people end up using is the same systems that they have always used. They know how to do it. It is familiar and comfortable. If it works, then why change it. Without mechanization wine landscapes are different from each other. Geographers love this because these differences challenge us to understand them and to explain why they are as they are.

NATURAL HAZARDS AND VITICULTURE

Viticulture is not just about how to grow crops. A good deal of problem solving is involved. Those of you who have trouble keeping house plants alive, or who have been forced into buying plastic plant substitutes, may already be well aware of that fact. Vintners are farmers. Like other farmers, they face weather-related, biotic, and economic threats to their livelihood. It is a tough industry and not all vintners and wineries are successful. We may not associate wineries and vineyards with Charles Darwin, but we should. We are talking about a process of selection (albeit not natural) and survival of the fittest. For vintners to be successful and to survive, they need to be able to adapt to the problems that life throws at them.

As in the evolution of species, changes to the environment have a significant impact on who survives and who doesn't. A change in the environment, whether natural, economic, or social, can create hazards for some and opportunities for others. After all, there is a great deal of potential profit in crisis. One man's hazard is another man's windfall. In fact, periodic disasters have been instrumental in reshaping the landscape of wine production over time.

Consider for example an extremely cold winter. The weather results in the loss of many vines and damage to equipment. The cost of this will be significant both during the year that follows and in succeeding seasons until the replanted grapes are in production. In the region where this occurred, the cost of the damage may force marginal vintners out of business. The land is still there. The vines are still there. What may not be there is the money to put all the pieces back together. For the economically healthy producer, the loss of competition may mean higher prices for their products. Just because there are fewer grapes being produced, does not mean there is less demand. It just means that more money will be paid for the grapes that are available. (OPEC simulates this process whenever they reduce oil exports.) This allows producers with greater financial resources to "weather" their own losses. If they have sufficient resources, some producers may even be able to benefit from the damage. They can expand their holdings by buying up vineyards that have been bankrupted by the winter losses. The die-off of plants may also give producers the opportunity, or excuse, to replant with new cultivars either to improve the quality or quantity of their grape production. Locally, the result is an increase in landholdings among the strongest producers. Outside the cold-affected region, the loss of competition and the higher pricing can increase profits. With those profits vintners can expand production into new areas, replant their fields, or improve their facilities. The result is more production area, more production, and possibly better production.

Some hazards occur with such frequency that we assume that they will occur and plan for them. We know some areas are very prone to flooding. In those areas we might opt for sod farming because grass does not mind the occasional inundation. Or we build levees in an attempt to keep out the flooding. In areas where early freezes are a common problem for vintners, we can either try to prevent the cold (as we discussed in the climate chapter) or we find inventive ways to deal with the problem while still making a profit. If we cannot prevent early frosts and are willing to live with the problem, a viable option for vintners might be iced wines (or eiswein). This is the "when life gives you lemons make lemonade" option. Iced wines are made from grapes left on the vine all winter. The constant freezing and thawing concentrates the sugars and produces a very sweet wine. This is a labor-intensive option that produces limited amounts of wine. As with other high-cost forms of agriculture, the additional costs can be offset by higher prices if the market is willing to pay. In this respect, the changing preferences of the wine market have done iced wines a disservice. The market for sweet wines is not what it once was. That said, the wine market is branching out. And if wine is anything like clothing, nothing will be out of fashion for too terribly long.

Not all of the environmental hazards that vintners face are weather related. Some are related to other causes. Animals can be a big problem because they like the same things about grapes that we do. Birds, rodents, and deer can literally make a meal out of a vintner's crop. Netting, a tall fence, or a few cats can often solve such problems. A far more costly and difficult problem is disease. Plant diseases can decimate a grape crop or the vines themselves. Consequently much has been written about plant disease and grapes. For our purposes we do not need to go wading into the literature. In fact, we do not need to look any further than the mirror. That is because the geographic concepts involved in understanding plant diseases are not all that different from the diseases that affect us.

At face value it may not seem there is much connection between the diseases that affect a local vintner's crop and a case of the chicken pox, but there are. That is because as geographers we are not looking at how disease affects plants, disease mortality, or how plant diseases can be cured. Rather we are looking at the geography of the disease. We are looking at where it occurs and how it moves. In that respect, diseases of all types have a great deal in common. Some diseases are strongly linked to certain kinds of environments; they are "endemic" to those places. Others move more freely and have well-understood mechanisms or pathways to their spread; they are "epidemic." In either case, it is the resulting patterns and pathways that geographers are interested in. You may not go to a geographer if you have a cold, but you might if you wanted to understand the pattern of AIDS diffusion or why certain kinds of cancers are more common in one location than in another.

Endemic diseases are linked to places with a certain type of environment. What that means is that we find the disease in places that have a certain set of environmental conditions. This is different from an epidemic which is an outbreak of a disease that is not linked to a place. Even some genetic diseases can have environmental influences that create distinct patterns. Whether a disease is endemic to a place often depends on whether that disease is "vectored." A vectored disease is one that requires an intermediary or carrier to transmit the disease, malaria being a good example. It is found in certain tropical locations because that is where its vector is found. Nonvectored diseases do not require a carrier. They can be transmitted from individual to individual, and can be found almost anywhere. The flu is a good example.

The problem with grapevines and disease is that all wine-producing regions are pretty similar environmentally. There may be local variations in environment, but most wine regions have an awful lot in common. As a result, a disease vector that can survive in one wine region may also be able to survive in others. Therefore, a disease that is endemic to one wine-producing region could end up being endemic to all wine-producing regions.

Grape reproductive processes also figure into the spread of disease. Unlike other crops, grapes are not typically planted in seed form. They could be, but more often than not they are reproduced through asexual propagation. Cuttings from the grape plant are grafted to existing root stock. This speeds up the reproductive process, gives great flexibility to the vintner, and makes up for the fact that the seeds are in the grapes and are thus lost in the crushing process. The problem from a disease standpoint is that if we are not careful, cuttings and root stock may carry disease. When we transport them, we end up being the disease vector. This is what authorities are trying to prevent at the airport when they force you to discard any agricultural produce or when they ask you if you have visited any farms in your travels.

A fungus may not be a disease, but the disease analogy fits them well. Fungi are the scourge of many crops. My particular favorite is powdery mildew. For years it has been the archenemy of my vegetable garden. As the name suggests, it is a fine, white, powdery mildew that forms on the leaves and stems of plants. It looks like a covering of powdered sugar, but the effect is disastrous. By the time you see it you might as well pack it in. Your garden is a goner.

Powdery mildew is an interesting example of the geography of disease. Although technically not a disease, it acts like one. Powdery mildew is not vectored; it is directly transmitted. In the early 1800s it spread like an epidemic through many of the world's vineyards. As geographers, powdery mildew is interesting because it challenges us to figure out how it was transmitted from one wine region to another and where it came from. Powdery mildew is one of a number of examples where people would appear to be culpable. The fact that powdery mildew and other plant pests spread rapidly with the spread of vine grafting strongly suggests that we were the vector of tainted grafts, and were the ultimate cause of their spread.

If we want to figure out where a fungus like powdery mildew comes from, it helps to go back to Charles Darwin. Darwin tells us that plants and animals adapt to the threats in their environment. Those that do not adapt do not survive. This can give us clues to where hazards like powdery mildew come from. Powdery mildew tends to have a dramatic impact on vinifera grapes coming out of Europe, but has less of an effect on vines indigenous to North America. If we assume that Darwin was right, the suggestion is that powdery mildew is from North America.

One important lesson from human diseases that we can apply here is that not all of them are bad. Some of them can be used to our benefit. For instance, one disease may be used as part of the inoculation process against another or to produce a variety of medicines. The analogy can be extended to our discussion of grapes and wine. Consider a distant relative of powdery mildew, the fungus botrytis. Unlike powdery mildew, botrytis does not kill its host. It affects only the fruit. This would seem like a big problem until we consider the specific way in which it does so. If left unchecked, botrytis will eventually turn all the grapes of a plant into shriveled, dusty balls. However, this occurs only if we let the fungus completely run its course. Up to a certain point, botrytis changes the chemistry of the fruit and gets rid of some of the moisture. Those changes have a positive impact on the taste and appearance of the resulting wine.

To take advantage of botrytis requires a strategy that is different than in most modern vineyards. Vintners cannot take advantage of the latest in farming equipment to reduce labor costs and produce high volumes of moderately priced wine. Nowhere is this better exemplified than in Sauterne. Sauterne is a small corner of Bordeaux that has become synonymous with the production of botrytis-affected wine. The regular fogs in the area create an ideal microclimate for the growth of botrytis, to the point where vintners in Sauterne have adapted to the botrytis to produce their wine. The vintners use multiple harvests, by hand, to pick the grapes that are botrytis affected but not *too* botrytis affected. This raises costs. The desiccation of the grapes lowers the wine production per acre of land. Together these factors make sauternes very expensive to produce. Great sauterne wineries like Château D'Yqem overcome this by producing great wines that people will pay a premium for. So while botrytis might not be for everyone, there are instances where it can be beneficial to certain types of wine production.

Probably the worst of the biotic threats affecting vintners is phylloxera. Phylloxera is to grapevines what the plague was to seventeenth-century Europeans. It is a disaster. It is a microscopic bug that attacks the roots of vines, eventually killing the plant. As it lives in the soil, it is susceptible to conditions within the soil. It does not like some soils. Soil flooding causes it some grief as well. Until the 1800s, isolation prevented its spread. Advances in transportation had the unfortunate side effect of allowing it to survive shipping and to spread in vine root stock. The result was a pandemic (a worldwide epidemic) that devastated wine production in the mid- to late 1800s and still influences the industry today.

Nowadays we have the science and technology to deal with biotic hazards such as phylloxera. A hundred years ago the situation was much different. Phylloxera cannot even be seen without a microscope. The other problem was that affected vines did not immediately die off. If they had, it would have at least given some clue as to the direction in which the problem was moving. Vintners found themselves fighting against an enemy they could not see. When they finally did understand the symptoms it was already too late. Better technology helps us to combat phylloxera. Early solutions that were used to defeat phylloxera proved to have significant downsides. Flooding vineyards to kill off the phylloxera had limited applicability. Early chemical solutions proved to be as dangerous to those applying them as they were to phylloxera. The one solution that did seem to work was grafting using American rootstock. This hints at its origins and was also part of the problem. The rootstock that was meant to combat phylloxera may have been instrumental in its spread.

As with the hypothetical example of the weather hazard described above, the economic effect of phylloxera was significant. The damage it caused and the cost of the solution had the effect of forcing out small producers, and reducing vineyard acreages through abandonment or by vintners changing to other crops. More than that, the loss of employment in the wine industry caused waves of emigration from wine-producing regions. At the time it was a genuine human tragedy. As the saying goes, time heals all wounds. Many of the people who left to find better lives found them in other parts of the world, and in doing so they brought their skills with them and did what they did best—produce wine. This is part of the history of wine and the spread of viticulture. It means that there is a good chance that your local vintner has a little phylloxera in his family tree. (Sorry—I couldn't resist.)

CALIFORNIA

California is synonymous with wine. Wine has been produced in California since the time of the first Spanish missions. Today, wine is the state's number-one cash crop. Part of the success of wine in California is due to its environment. Each valley seems to provide vintners with a different combination of climate, topography, and soil. Given that diversity, we can find *terroirs* appropriate to the full range of wine grape varietals. The fact that so many different wine *terroirs* exist within a relatively short drive of the San Francisco Bay makes them convenient for study and for the wine tourists that flock to the region by the thousands each week.

If we played a game of word association for "California," some people might be tempted to say something about warm weather, palm trees, Pacific sunsets, earthquakes, and surfing.

Those would probably not be wine people. The stereotype of Southern California and its culture is based on the Los Angeles basin and San Diego. Someone more familiar with Northern California might be more likely to refer to the remark attributed to Mark Twain: "The coldest winter that I ever spent was a summer in San Francisco."

The weather and climate of California is strongly influenced by the Pacific Ocean and the California Current. The cold water of the current follows the West Coast from Canada to Mexico. In doing so it mixes the ocean waters off the coast producing upwelling and a rich environment for sea creatures. The current also chills the air that passes over it. The result is that the coast is cooler than areas farther inland. Even along the central California coastline, in places such as Santa Cruz, Monterey, and Santa Ynez, the cold water of the Pacific brings lower temperatures. Because the relative humidity of air will drop as the temperature rises, California is drier away from the coastline. The fogs that are prominent along the north coast are partly a product of the California Current. Warm air passing over the cold water of the current is chilled, increasing its humidity to the point at which water vapor can condense to produce a fog. The resulting fogs can be quite substantial and a significant problem for transportation in the region.

For vintners the coastal fogs are a good thing, and they have two positive influences on wine production in the region. First, they reduce heating during the summer. The fogs cool the air over the vineyards until the daytime winds disperse them or the rising heat of the day evaporates them away. The net affect is less exposure to the scorching temperatures inherent to a

California summer. This allows for the planting of cooler climate grapes that need a long growing season but not scalding weather. The other positive effect of the fogs is in providing moisture for plants. On cold nights the surface temperatures can be significantly lower than the damp, foggy air blowing in off the ocean. As fog comes in contact with cold surfaces, water can condense on them in the form of dew. In humid climates we might not consider dew an important water source for plants. In more arid climates that moisture may be very important to the survival of plants. In fact, plants that are indigenous to fog-prone regions will evolve through time to take advantage of that water resource.

A concern of residents along the length of the California coastline is earthquakes. Coastal California is at the boundary of the North American and Pacific plates. The movement of the plates is the root cause of the earthquake activity that poses a significant hazard to wineries and to the region as a whole. If we look at the movement of the plates over millions of years our focus changes from earthquakes to landforms. That is because over geologic time scales the plate movements have reshaped the earth's surface along the entire West Coast of North America. In northern and central California the result is a landscape of interconnected alluvial valleys and long ridgelines that run roughly parallel to the coast. This geology is extremely relevant to viticulture in the region. The ridges serve to direct and to trap air coming off the Pacific Ocean. Surface runoff from the ridges carries eroded soil and nutrients into the valleys. The combination of the influences of climate and the offshore currents creates the environmental diversity that California vintners thrive on.

The diversity of wine-growing environments is most pronounced in the area north of San Francisco. The confluence of the Pacific, San Francisco Bay, the long valleys, differences in elevation, and exposure to fog and winds creates the means by which each valley will have a noticeably different *terroir*. Napa is just one valley to the east of Sonoma. Calistoga is in the same valley but is slightly higher in elevation than nearby St. Helena. The Russian River valley viticulture area is just across the valley from Chalk Hill. There are many other recognizable Northern California wine regions that we could use as examples. Assuming that the traffic is not too bad, all of them are within a half hour's drive of one another.

There are other parts of California where wine is produced: in the foothills of the Sierra Nevada Mountains on the east side of the Central Valley, and in the Salinas River valley inland from Monterey. The vineyards in these areas are not as extensive because locations whose conditions are suited to high-quality wine production are limited. In some instances conditions are better suited to varietals used in the production of raisins or table grapes.

In California they do not just cultivate vines. They cultivate people, too. If there is any place where viticulture and enology are raised to a science it is in California. At universities such as the University of California at Davis, Sonoma State University, and California State University at Fresno, scientists produce innovations that their students take into the "real world" of wine. The fact that these universities include programs in viticulture and enology is based on their close proximity to California's wine regions. Because these are state universities, and as wine production is important to California's economy, these universities have a vested interest in taking their research out into the field. Their outreach activities and their students make California rich in human resources for wine. We may not be able to see those resources when the tour buses drop us off at the vineyards. In fact, we may decry the new science of winemaking, since our romantic notions of wine do not normally include images of technicians in lab coats, stainless steel vats, and wineries that resemble oil refineries. We will, however, taste their influence on the wines of California.

Chapter 8

WINE AND GEOGRAPHIC INFORMATION SYSTEMS

When I first started graduate school way back in the Stone Age, high-tech mapping applications and the use of spatial analysis systems were just beginning to become popular in geography. They had been around for quite a while. However, it was not until the proliferation of personal computers that they started to become popular. Low-cost personal computers meant that geography departments could afford to stock custom-built computer labs. These labs soon became the domain of a new generation of students who grew up on the computer. The result has been the demise of the pen-and-ink cartography (mapmaking) that I did to make beer money in college. Today not even the drafting tables remain.

The reason I bring this up is that back then, computer cartography and geographic information systems (GIS) inhabited a world completely separate from that of wine and its geography. At the same time I was rushing off to assist John Dome with his wine courses, the "computer geeks" among the graduate students were heading off to the computer lab. After class I would go to the lab so that they could help me with the computing assignments. We would work on our homework and take care of the leftovers from that night's wine class. Other than the wine that we drank (and my homework), there was little that connected the two.

Today it seems that every geography department in the world is cranking out students who are pulling down impressive salaries doing GIS work. Some of them are even connecting to the world of wine through the use of GIS, global positioning systems (GPS), and remote-sensing technology. This infusion of geographic technology is a great thing for the wine industry. It is especially valuable when determining where to site new vineyards and what to plant within them. The only unfortunate side effect is that it is forcing people like me to go back and learn to use technology that we so readily dismissed eons ago.

WHAT IS GIS?

Geography can help to answer important questions for vintners. Where should we develop new vineyards? What grapes are the best suited for a given location? Where should we market our wines? We can answer these questions through trial and error. However, trial and error costs time and money. New technologies yield quality information, which we can analyze and use to make better decisions. We can still make mistakes, but with any luck we make them more infrequently.

Geographic information systems have developed over the past two decades to become one of the most important tools in geography. It is crucial for conducting geographic research and is the meal ticket for a generation of geographers. It is a technology that has quickly entered the mainstream and has provided geographers with a wealth of employment opportunities.

To see an example of a GIS, log on to your favorite Internet search engine and use its mapping link to create a simple location map. What created that map is a GIS. Simply put, GIS uses computerized mapping and databases to take information and assign it a location. When we tell the computer an address, it locates it on a map. That same GIS can then be used to find restaurants, hotels, or gas stations on the map. The reason this is possible is because the addresses of these businesses appear in a database somewhere. Those addresses are used to connect the data to another database that has the roads. Put the two together and voilà! We have a map that includes whatever we wish to locate programmed into the GIS.

GIS systems are available online and have even become a selling point for automobiles. Any car that has a dashboard screen with maps and location information has a GIS. The only difference between the in-dash GIS and the one online is that the GIS system in the car does not have an address. Because the car moves we need another bit of technology to tell the GIS where the car is located. This information comes to the car courtesy of a global positioning system sensor. GPS systems use multiple satellites to triangulate our location and elevation. The GIS provides the mapped data while the GPS tells the computer where we are on the map. The result is a GIS/GPS system that can tell us where we are and where we are going.

Touring wine country in a nice car we can use our in-dash GIS/GPS to locate every vineyard, every winery, as well as all of the hotels, restaurants, gas stations, and tour companies that appear in the phone book. If the phone company has an address, it will appear in a GIS database somewhere. The system can even tell us the fastest routes to our destination by calculating the distance and the speed limits on the different types of roads we will be traveling on. If our travels included a flight on a fairly new airplane then we probably watched a GIS/GPS system in action. The onboard display that cycles through maps of the airplane's location, elevation information, and airspeed is yet another example of a GIS/GPS in action.

Within the wine industry the use of GIS is much more than simply a way to get tourists to a local winery. For vintners, the more profound and profitable use of GIS is in site selection. Site selection asks us two basic geographic questions: What use would be best for a given piece of land? Or, what piece of land would be best for a given use? As geographers, site selection is something we tend to be good at because it is all about making good geographic decisions. The use of GIS simply makes those decisions easier and better.

Consider a GIS that is programmed not with information on restaurants, gas stations, and hotels but with incredibly detailed information on soil types, temperature, rainfall, topography, and sun exposure. Then add data on grape varietals, their ideal growing conditions, the volume of wine they produce, and the value of that wine. Put the datasets together and we can match the fields in our vineyard with the best grapes to grow there. By expanding the database to include existing land uses, land value, and land-use regulations, we can use our GIS to identify any available land that might be good for starting a new vineyard.

In older wine-producing regions the use of GIS for site selection is not common. That is because hundreds of years of wine production have provided all the answers about what to grow and where to grow it. The vineyards were in place before the technology was invented. Site-selection uses for a GIS will also be less common in areas where there simply is no land available for vineyard expansion. GIS applications are in use in such areas, but for something other than site selection. They can be used to track information on the existing vineyards. In fact, vintners who like using the technology can have a GIS track every vine, its type, planting date, and productivity. Most vintners will not go to that extreme. Rather they will use a GIS to track that information for individual fields or for rows of grapes within those fields.

To see GIS used to its fullest, one must go to wine regions that are young and growing. There GIS is much more than a means of data storage and retrieval. The availability of land and the limited history of wine production give us an opportunity to apply the information that GIS provides. That information can be used to guide land purchases and vineyard expansion as well as to influence planting decisions. The use of GIS can assist in making decisions that will affect wine quality and vineyard profitability for years to come.

One of the biggest concerns in the use of a GIS is the quality of information that is put in. A GIS is only as good as its data. Garbage input results in garbage output. Luckily there are many good data sources out there. Government agencies and private providers can yield a wealth of good mapable data. Some of that information has been collected and placed in databases. In addition, some types of environmental information on soils, vegetation, and so on, exist in the form of aerial photographs or satellite imagery.

We loosely refer to aerial photography and satellite imagery as being "remotely sensed" data. It is data that we acquire without being in direct contact with it. Remote sensing has grown from its roots as a product of the military to be our window on the environment of the earth as well as the other planets in our solar system.

Even before the first aerial reconnaissance missions in World War I, people recognized the value of a "bird's-eye view" of things. By simply changing the point of view, a great deal of additional information could be revealed. Over the years, remote sensing grew from simple aerial photography to placing digital imaging systems, the precursors of our digital cameras, on satellites. By going digital, remote sensing not only changed our vantage point, it expanded what we could see by gathering information invisible to the naked eye.

When remote sensing began to pioneer the use of digital imaging systems, it went well beyond what we can see. Our eyes are biologic systems for detecting certain kinds of electromagnetic energy. What our eyes can detect is, however, very limited. The electromagnetic spectrum includes an incredibly broad range of energy types that differ based on their wavelength. The visible part of the spectrum is only a tiny portion of all electromagnetic radiation. The rest cannot be seen without the help of technology.

Our digital cameras use an electronic sensor that detects the same wavelengths that we can see. In other words, they take in the same information that our eyes do. There are imaging systems that allow us to look at other wavelengths. This is quite useful as some of the wavelengths that we cannot see provide information that a farmer or vintner would find quite useful. At certain wavelengths, minute differences in soil moisture become readily apparent, or where a healthy leaf can be distinguished from one that is just beginning to see the effects of disease, possibly early enough for the observer to do something about it. The right kind of imaging systems can sense heat and cold air drainage, and thus allow us to measure microclimatic variations in the landscape. By combining remote sensing and other types of data, a GIS can be made even more useful for site selection.

We can include information from a variety of sources in creating a good GIS. To make climate part of our GIS we can include information from nearby weather stations. If we are lucky, we could also include heat summation information if it is readily available. We could then link up our GIS to information on the climatic or heat summation preferences of grape varietals. As part of understanding the local *terroirs* we could also include soil information and topography in our GIS. Thankfully this information is readily available in most developed countries where a governmental entity monitors soil and is engaged in topographic mapping. Such agencies disseminate information to the general public as a service to assist farmers and other individuals who might benefit from that information. In the United States those organizations are the Natural Resources Conservation Service (NRCS) and the United States Geologic Survey (USGS). Formerly called the Soil Conservation Service, the NRCS has soil surveys for almost all of the United States except for a few isolated parts of the Rockies and Alaska. Those surveys provide very detailed soil information. Mostly these are in book form. However, recent surveys and survey revisions have been put online. In that way those of us who have broadband and a whole lot of time can access them (the files are *huge*). The USGS also has topographic maps at various scales for nearly all parts of the United States. Some of this information provided comes in the form of maps that can be downloaded for immediate use. Like the NRCS, some of that information is provided in digital forms that allow it to be incorporated into GIS applications.

Even with the available data sources on climate, soils, and topography, it is still very helpful to obtain the advice of experts. Major wine companies employ such individuals. For the rest of us there is agricultural extension, which is part of the mission of many universities. If a university near you has a school of agriculture it typically has an extension system that employs specialists and faculty to help farmers become even better farmers. For vintners, extension agents are a source of information on environmental issues, agricultural concerns, and for improvements in production. At the university, faculty and research scientists may be busy conducting tests of grape varietals, treating wine pests, or trying to develop new grape hybrids. This work is a natural outgrowth of the promotion and tenure process. The impact of that work is that it provides a base of knowledge available to all vintners. This levels the playing field by giving small vintners access to research they themselves would not be able to fund.

Through the work of extension offices, the results of on-campus research can be brought to the attention of the professionals working in the field. In this way extension offices function as a bridge from the classroom and laboratory to the "real world." It is through this bridge that computer technology and geographic information systems entered the world of wine. Even today, innovative GIS applications still travel from classrooms to application in the field through the work of local extension offices.

OREGON AND WASHINGTON STATE

If we want to change careers and have the financial resources to open a vineyard, where would we go? There are places that have proven to be great environments for wine production. Starting somewhere like Napa or Sonoma would give us a head start on our marketing. The problem is that their reputation and history of viticulture means that all the good land will already be in production. We would have to buy an existing vineyard.

If we want to live the dream of being a vintner but want to start from scratch, we might want to move up the coast a bit to Oregon or Washington. The climate will be different. We may not be able to grow some grapes that are adapted to Mediterranean conditions, but there are plenty of cultivars from Marine West Coast climates that would work well there. More important, Oregon and Washington offer much more in the way of available land. We can convert existing farmland to vineyards and be in control of everything from the very start.

Before we go running off to the Pacific Northwest with a checkbook and a dream, we need to understand that grape growing will not work well everywhere in those states. We must appreciate the topography of those states, the rain shadow effect, and what these things mean for wine production. A detailed climate map of the Pacific Northwest will illustrate the fact that climatic conditions vary greatly as we move from west to east across Oregon and Washington. These variations are due to the rain shadow effect.

As in California, the coastlines of Oregon and Washington are strongly influenced by the Pacific Ocean and the California Current. The westerly winds coming off of the Pacific are cool and damp throughout the year, which means that coastal locations are not ideal for wine grape production.

This is where the rain shadow effect comes into play. Paralleling the coastline are the Coast Range and Olympic mountains. The cool moist air coming off of the Pacific changes as it is pushed up the mountains. Its temperature drops and relative humidity increases, resulting in substantial amounts of rainfall on the windward side of these mountains. There is so much rainfall that some locations have a temperate rain forest as well as some of the highest average rainfall totals in North America. As the air passes down the leeward side it loses some of its moisture and is significantly warmer. Consequently the Willamette Valley and Puget Sound Lowland have climates that are different from the coast a few miles away.

The rain shadow effect occurs because of differing rates at which air cools as it rises. As air rises it cools at a rate of around 6 degrees Fahrenheit per 1,000 feet of elevation change, and does so until precipitation occurs. Then the rate of change drops to around 3 degrees per 1,000 feet. On the way down the leeward side of the mountain the air will heat at 6 degrees per 1,000 feet, stopping the precipitation in the process. So, if there was rain for even a part of the passage up the mountain, the air will be warmer and drier when it reaches the valley floor on the other side of the mountain. This is why many of the world's deserts are found on the leeward side of large mountain chains.

The rain shadow affect means that the Willamette Valley and Puget Sound Lowland will be drier and slightly warmer than the coast. The same thing happens in a more pronounced fashion when the air passes over the much higher Cascade Range of mountains farther inland. The result is that as we pass from west to east across Oregon and Washington we begin with cool wet conditions on the coastal lowlands and end up with near-desert conditions on the Columbia Plateau.

The rain shadow effect gives us a range of possibilities to establish vineyards in Oregon and Washington. The first possibilities are in the valleys just inland of the Coast Range and Olympic Mountains. Of these, the Willamette Valley has become especially prominent in the wine industry. A growing number of vineyards are slowly displacing the feed crops and dairying that have traditionally existed there. To recall von Thunen, what we are seeing is a decision motivated by profit. In the Willamette Valley today, vineyards have a better profit potential than dairies or small family farms. There is also an element to the wine industry that goes beyond simple profit, and these motivations are at work in the Willamette Valley. A culture of, and an aesthetic appeal to, wine is evident in the development of the new wineries. The wineries celebrate the farming culture of the valley in their architecture. The reuse of old barns for new wineries may be an economic decision, but the construction of new wineries that look like old barns pays tribute to the farming heritage of the valley.

The downside of the Willamette Valley, as well as the Puget Sound Lowland farther north, is that these areas are already developed and will have higher prices. Urbanization in the valleys is also a problem. Thankfully, Oregon and Washington are two of the most progressive states in the country at regulating the growth of their urban areas. They are nowhere near as developed or as pricey as Napa and Sonoma. If, however, we would like to go where no winemaker has gone before, the Willamette Valley may still not be a great fit for us.

To venture off the beaten path in our search for the perfect spot to live the dream of being vintners, we may want to try the Columbia Plateau. In Oregon, most of the plateau is rather cool for wine grape production due to its high elevation. In Washington, the elevation of the plateau is lower and the conditions are thus warmer than in Oregon. They are not warm by California standards but they can produce cooler weather varietals like pinot noir and Riesling. Given the wide open spaces and relative lack of development, there are opportunities for budding wine entrepreneurs to develop vineyards in the Yakima, Columbia, and Walla Walla valleys. Because our dreams of owning a vineyard may come with a budget, eastern Washington may be just the place we are looking for.

For those individuals with the determination to become vintners, there are opportunities out there. More than that, resources and technologies exist to help budding vintners to make good geographic decisions about where to start and what to grow. Whether it is remote sensing and geographic information systems, or scientific research and advice dispensed through agricultural extension offices, there has rarely been a better time or environment for those looking to get into the business of growing grapes and making wine.

Chapter 9

WINEMAKING
AND GEOGRAPHY

When I was the graduate assistant for John Dome's wine course, he had a night each semester that was devoted to the subject of dessert wines. I remember the evening rather well, but not because of the lecture material. Part of my job as John's graduate assistant was to "dispose" of any wine that remained after the class was over. For opened bottles this meant pouring out the remaining wine and recycling the bottles. For unopened bottles, "disposing" had a very different meaning. On the dessert wine night I remember sitting at my desk and puzzling over what to do with all of the unopened bottles of wine. I had to borrow an extra book bag in order to get all the bottles of port, sherry, and sauterne back to my apartment. What I also remember is trying my best to be inconspicuous while toting two book bags full of wine bottles past the campus police station on the walk home.

What does this have to do with the geography of wine? If anything it is a testament to how taste preferences can change over time and how they can be specific to a culture and a place. Sweetness used to be prized in wine. Some cultures may still feel that way. It is also a testament to how winemaking can produce very different results with very subtle changes to the process.

The human sense of taste is incredibly important to the wine industry. However, the sensation of taste is not geographic. Although the mechanics of taste are constant, how we interpret taste varies from location to location. The sensation of taste is a physiological process common to almost all people. What is not common is which tastes people like and dislike. Taste preference is not just a physical response, it is a learned response. Taste preference can be particular to a culture or place. When we start talking about people and places, geographers have a lot to say on the matter.

Taste is in part a learned response, and will be influenced by what we eat on a regular basis. If we turned the clock back a hundred years or so, what we ate was very specific to where we lived. Even today, isolated societies are limited in their exposure to food items and tastes from other parts of the world.

The link between food and places is part of the context behind the concept of *terroir*. If we can associate foods with specific environments, we can do the same with taste. It affects what foods we are used to and how we perceive the taste of foods. It may even have an impact on what we label as food.

REGIONAL WINEMAKING VARIATIONS

The sense of taste is universal. To some extent so is winemaking, regardless of the location. Given the commonalities in production it should come as no surprise that the equipment is quite common as well. The global market for winemaking equipment is such that there is now a high degree of standard-ization. In some cases, traditional winemaking techniques and equipment persist. This is especially true where winemaking is an integral part of the local culture. Even in those areas, tradi-tional techniques are sometimes relegated to display produc-tion, special events, and ceremonies.

Some forms of winemaking, however, have traditionally been different. Over time, unique region-specific processes for making wine have persisted to the point where the process has become intertwined with the place. In an earlier chapter we saw an example of this in the discussion of sauterne the wine and Sauterne the place. The link can become so ingrained in our thinking that we find it strange when the product is made somewhere else. That is because there are wines and wine regions where variations in the basic winemaking process have become institutionalized. Champagne, Jerez, Oporto, Madeira, and Marsala are places where the processes of wine-making are different from the norm. They are also good exam-ples of how the techniques for making wine become so associated with their origins that the place name is the wine name. Legal systems now protect the links between certain wines and places. One may take a cynical approach to this and label it market protectionism. We can also see such measures as means of protecting the unique associations between places and products. In that sense, the laws are protecting the geographical quirks of winemaking.

Madeira is a great story of wine geography and how a place became synonymous with the wine it produces. The island of Madeira is part of Portugal. It is one of many small volcanic islands off the western coasts of Spain, Portugal, and Morocco. Today it is one of the southernmost locations in the European Union and a destination for tourists looking to enjoy the island's warm weather, pristine beaches, and wooded mountains. In the age of sailing ships, the prevailing winds made Madeira the last stop before trading vessels made the Atlantic crossing. Because high air pressure and lack of wind to the north made the Azores a poor choice for sailing ships, and the Cape Verde islands to the south were too hot and dry to make a good watering stop, Madeira became a regular stop for ships looking to top off their water supply. Those same ships provided a ready market for the island's wine. Trade agreements between the English and Portuguese helped to cement Madeira's importance in the transatlantic trade.

Madeira wine is fortified by brandy or by cane spirit. The link with sugar cane is based on the regular rainfall and warm temperatures that allowed for sugar cane production on Madeira. By accident or design, the fortification of Madeira wine helped it survive the trip across the Atlantic. As the crossing was made via the tropics, the heat would cause normal wines to go bad in a hurry. The additional alcohol content provided through fortification allowed Madeira to survive the long periods of tropical heat. Madeira sales in Europe would have been limited due to competition from other wine-producing regions, and it also would have been rather difficult to transport Madeira wine against the prevailing winds. However, it did make Madeira a very popular drink in the colonies. It was the only wine other than port that New World colonists were likely to get that would still be fit to drink. More than two hundred years have changed the nature of transatlantic trade, but what has not changed is the link between Madeira and the winemaking technique which has flourished there.

WINEMAKING AS AN INDUSTRY

Winemaking is a form of processing. Although we may shudder at the thought of it, this makes winemaking an industrial activity. In processing we take raw materials and change their form so that they are more useful and valuable. This is essentially what we are doing when we make wine; we take grapes and change their form into something that is more useful and valuable to us. Winemaking as processing means that a winery has a lot in common with a cannery or a lumber mill.

Comparing a winery, a cannery, and a lumber mill may seem rather ludicrous, but from a geographic perspective they share certain features. All three take products from nature and alter their form. In doing so, the products lose a great deal of weight. In winemaking we are disposing of the grape solids. In a cannery we are removing the parts of the fish or crab that are not marketable. In a lumber mill we are disposing of bark and scrap woods. Such processing activities are weight losing. That gives them a common geography.

The geography of processing, and of weight-losing products, is focused heavily on the issue of transportation. Why should we pay to transport materials that are thrown away? This may not amount to much with wine, but consider a mining operation. There will be a huge amount of worthless waste rock for a very small amount of valuable metals. Why transport waste materials?

Cost and profit dictate that we process near the resource. We build the lumber mill near the forest, the cannery at the fishing port, and the winery near the vineyards.

The other issue that is important to understanding processing and transportation is spoilage. Spoilage may not be a major concern in the lumber industry or in mining, but consider a cannery. It is ideal if I can get crab that is alive and healthy until the time I drop it into a pot of boiling water. But if I have to buy crab that is already processed, then I want crab that was alive and healthy until the moment it was cooked at the cannery. The longer it takes the crab to get to a sterile environment, the more the health and safety of the meat becomes an issue. Given the risks involved, I would rather not take any chances.

As consumers, we tend to pay a good deal of attention to spoilage issues related to meat. This is simply because meat that has gone bad during transport poses a very serious health risk. When grapes get "funky" during transport the issue of consumer health is not as pronounced. When grapes go bad the cause is usually premature fermentation. As we already discussed, fermentation is part of the winemaking process, but we like to be able to control the yeasts that do the work. Trusting quality winemaking to whatever microbes might be floating around in a vineyard is unrealistic. Grapes can be treated with sulfur dioxide to kill off the wild yeasts. Yeasts specifically suited to the process of winemaking can then be used.

We expect to see wineries located near vineyards. Historically, spoilage during transportation dictated that vintners sold their produce to local wineries. This provided an incentive for vintners to produce their own wine. Wine production gave them control over the finished product. It also gave them the financial benefits—and unfortunately the liabilities—of wine production. The control of production and profits has been the basis for the combined ownership of vineyards and wineries. Refrigeration has changed this pattern, and has made the long-distance transportation of grapes viable. As a result, a winery and a vineyard can be physically separate, although there are still financial and creative incentives for the combined ownership of vineyard and winery. From a geographic perspective we appreciate this because it gives wine a local connection. Without it, *terroir* and place would be far less important to wine.

Transportation is an important issue for the wine industry. Transportation is getting cases of wine bottles from the producer, to the distributor, and to the consumer as quickly, safely, and economically as possible. Transportation costs are key variables in making good geographic decisions concerning processing and the production of wine. In spite of its importance, transportation is part of the wine industry that we typically think little about. It goes on behind the scenes. Although we pore over a wine label to glean as much information as we can about the wine and where it is produced, we ignore the information, if there is any, on the company responsible for getting the wine to us. Unless there is a problem, the process escapes our notice.

Over time, transportation has been an incredibly important factor in the geography of wine. As a liquid, wine posed major transportation problems due to its form and its weight. It was difficult to move around. Fermentation was a further complication.

Grapes would rapidly begin to ferment, limiting their transportability. Before the advent of airtight containers, wines could continue fermentation during the transportation process. Bottling helped to limit fermentation during transport, but it created other complications. Early wine bottles were fragile, and as such, breakage during transport was a major economic concern. This was especially true because the best roads of the day were cobbled.

Given the perishability of the product, there was a significant advantage in producing wine near the marketplace. As we shall see later in the book, transportation problems meant that wine regions developed in conjunction with the markets that they served. To sell wine to more distant markets a way had to be found to stabilize it so that it would not go bad during transport. As with Madeira, this could be accomplished by increasing the alcohol content of the wine. At a high enough level the alcohol content stops the fermentation process. Buyers close to the wineries or with very good access could get good low-alcohol wines. Buyers at a greater distance were forced to resort to high-alcohol wines and liquors. At even longer distances or in areas without good trade access, buyers turned to other types of alcohol from locally grown products.

The shipping of heavy products, especially those prone to spoilage, has traditionally been difficult. The poor quality of early road systems only compounded the problem. Thus, water-based transport became the best means of shipping wine, and remained so into the late-nineteenth century. Water-based transport is still the most efficient means of transporting high-volume and high-weight products, such as automobiles. The importance of water-based transport was a factor that made canal construction economically viable. Canals allowed for the safe and smooth shipment of large volumes/weights of goods. Over time, railroads replaced canals as transportation options for agriculture and industry. Where canals still are in operation, their use has become recreational. In fact, barge tours have become quite popular for tourists who want to experience travel in the slow lane.

Canals and oceangoing transportation are still relevant in some types of trade. In terms of wine, some of that relevance has been lost over time. Railroads, highways, and air freight have overtaken water-based transport in the movement of wine from producers to consumers. In some cases the move to more rapid forms of transportation has spawned interesting results. A case in point is in the distribution of Beaujolais nouveau. Beaujolais is at the far southern end of the Burgundy wine region. Although technically part of Burgundy it has a climate that is distinct from its more northern neighbors. The climate is such that the gamay grape thrives in Beaujolais and it is that grape which is the basis for Beaujolais nouveau. What makes the wine interesting both from a transport and a winemaking perspective is that it is not aged. The wine is fermented and is transported to market as quickly as possible. Over time the release of the wine has been standardized to the third Thursday in November. Upon release, a deluge of wine is shuffled off to awaiting trucks which rush the wine to air freight terminals for the first available flights overseas. The wine is being poured by consumers literally within hours of its release. The cost of air freight on a pound-for-pound basis is far in excess of any other form of transport. As such, it is usually limited to products that are high value but with little volume or weight. The price that people are willing to pay for the first Beaujolais nouveau of the season offsets the increased cost of such transportation.

Although overtaken by other forms of transportation, the modern geography of wine was shaped by shipping. As we have seen, the importance of cities such as Nantes and Bordeaux was based on transportation. Goods from the interior, including wine, were shipped downriver to the ports for export to foreign markets. The ports became market centers and the focus of foreign investment. In the world of wine, two of the classic examples have been the ports of Oporto and Cadiz.

OPORTO AND CADIZ

Oporto and Cadiz may not mean much to people outside Portugal and Spain. They are modest-sized port cities on the Atlantic coast, and at one time were important trading centers with significant wealth derived from trade with Portuguese and Spanish colonies in the New World. The wealth of that past is reflected in the architectural heritage of the two cities. Even so, they are not well known to people outside the region. More recognizable to wine lovers are the exports from those cities, because these cities are where port and sherry have traditionally been exported to the world's wine consumers.

Port and sherry are good examples of the links that were forged between wines, the places that they are produced, and water-based transport. Port and sherry are produced through techniques that are distinct from those used to produce standard red or white wines. Port and sherry are wines that are fortified with additives. They make a rather interesting subject of geographic study because the type of fortification has become synonymous with the places where they developed.

The term "port" is derived from Oporto, the name of the Portuguese city from which it is exported. Oporto is near the mouth of the Duoro River valley. The Duoro River is important to port production because it is at the heart of northern Portugal's wine-producing regions. In many places the south-facing slopes leading down to the river are terraced with vineyards. The river itself was the focus of wine transportation to the lodges in Oporto. In fact, some port labels still bear images of the small flat-bottomed sailing vessels, *barcos rabelas,* used to transport the grapes to the lodges. Thanks to flood-control projects and locks along its length, the river is now tame enough to support small river cruise ships. The companies that ply the river advertise that it is the most beautiful river in Europe. This may be debatable since just about every cruise line in Europe says the same thing about the rivers they cruise. What is not debatable is that the cruises now give tourists the opportunity to see the river, its towns, and to experience the region and its wines.

The link between Oporto and the port trade is not accidental. Oporto is a good example of what geographers refer to as a "break of bulk" point. The *barcos* that used to run up and down the length of the Duoro were well adapted to the river. Their design would be far from ideal in the swells of the open ocean. Prior to the modern flood-control system, ships capable of oceangoing transport were not capable of traveling more than a few miles upriver. This made Oporto the point where goods were taken ashore, warehoused, lodged, and then reloaded for the next leg of their journey. Active break of bulk points such as Oporto developed into trading communities and, in some cases, large cities.

Oporto is more than just a point of trade. It is in Oporto where the port "lodges" are located. It is in the lodges that Oporto takes on an interesting twist that we can see in photographs of the city. If we search for images of Oporto on the Internet, we find views of a city which is pure Portugal in appearance. The exceptions to this are the English-sounding company names that are plastered all over the walls, roofs, and billboards of the port lodges. The English names reflect an interesting history of Portuguese wine exports to England. At certain points in its history, Oporto has been a primary supplier of wine to England. That trade brought English investment and investors to Oporto. The high alcohol content resulting from the fortifying process helped port survive transport to England. Not only did the English investors leave their names to the port lodges, the English influenced the development of the wine itself.

Geographically and historically there were good reasons for the English to be active in the port trade. While England and France were squabbling, as they did throughout much of history, the French wine ports of Nantes and Bordeaux were off-limits. Moving farther south, the next major port with access to significant amounts of wine was Oporto. Unlike ports in northern Spain, which was also often in conflict with the

English, Oporto had the Duoro River, which provided access to the wine regions of the interior and gave Oporto access to wine and a basis for some very profitable trade.

Although the wine may be different, the history and geography of sherry has a lot in common with port. "Sherry" is a bastardization of Jerez, which is short for Jerez de la Frontera, the town just inland from the port of Cadiz where the sherry industry is based. Sherry became part of the wine trade later than port. In fact, the rise of sherry was as a competitor to port. Port is made by fortifying wine with brandy. In doing so the fermentation process is stopped. Given the variations from year to year in the grape harvest and the difficulty involved in standardizing the fortification process, a great deal of variation in port was possible. Sometimes the process resulted in a product of excellence. For some lesser producers, it often resulted in a hit-or-miss experience. Sherry is produced using the Solera system, in which young wines are blended with older wines as part of the aging process. Blending prolongs fermentation producing higher alcohol levels. Blending wines over many years in the Solera system also provides for a consistency of taste, an important factor in the marketing of wine.

Sherry becomes significant in the wine trade after the fall of Napoleon. British troops under Lord Wellington (the man who defeated Napoleon at Waterloo) campaigned in Portugal and Spain. Cape Trafalgar, after which the battle was named, is just south of Cadiz. With British troops in the region, it would have been natural for sherry to have come to the attention of the British wine market. As Cadiz is the closest major Spanish port with export potential for wine, peace between Spain and Britain would have made Jerez and sherry an economically viable competitor for Oporto and port. As such, it too would have been an area ripe for British investors and investment.

The English influence draws sherry and port together. Geographically, however, the places that produce those wines are very different. Andalusia, the region of Spain in which Jerez is located, was the last part of the Iberian Peninsula to be held by the Moors. The Moorish influence is reflected in the region's architecture, especially in the regional capital of Sevilla. Little of that cultural influence is visible in Oporto. Cadiz was also one of the last ports of call for Spanish ships heading off to the New World. So its culture and heritage are visible in many of the areas colonized by the Spanish.

The two regions are also different in their physical geography. Oporto is in a region of rolling hills climatically similar to areas of Northern California. The influence of the Atlantic helps to moderate the weather, providing winter rains and keeping temperatures at reasonable levels during the summer. The landscape of Jerez is relatively flat and barren with a limestone-rich soil that is almost white in some areas. The Atlantic Ocean influences the winter weather in Jerez, bringing rains and cooler temperatures. The winter is short, however. The proximity of Jerez to northern Africa and the Sahara Desert means that summer in Jerez is significantly hotter and drier than in Oporto. When the winds shift in the spring, Jerez goes from cool and damp to oven-like in very short order.

Port and sherry share a common history of British influence and trade. They are also often grouped together under the banner of fortified wines. That being said, the two wine regions are as diverse as the wines they produce. Although you may see them together on the wine list of your favorite restaurant, behind each is an interesting and unique story of the geography of wine.

Chapter 10

WINE DIFFUSION, COLONIALISM, AND POLITICAL GEOGRAPHY

In the beginning there was the ancestor of *Vitis vinifera*. Like most grapes, they were good. That was a few thousand years ago somewhere in the Caucasus Mountains. So how the heck did they spread all over the globe? It is this kind of question that geographers just love. Why? Because it allows us to do what we do best. We look at where something started, where it finished, the path it took, how it changed en route, and the mechanism(s) that took it from start to finish. It is a geographic detective story. Some geographers like to do this with music. Some do it with sports. Others like to do it with more academically lofty subjects such as, to name a few, language and religion. We are doing it with wine.

In approaching this detective story, we need to keep in mind a few important ground rules. First, we must distinguish between the movement of the grapes, the knowledge of how to grow them, the knowledge of how to make wine out of them, and the movement of the people who have that knowledge. We are looking at the diffusion of people, things, and ideas. Each element is important to understanding the travels of grapes and wine through place and time.

WINE FROM ITS ORIGINS

The early production of wine was as a natural by-product of grape harvests, because in climates where grapes grow, summer and early-fall temperatures are high enough for fermentation to take place. Without airtight containers, refrigeration, or a means of killing the yeasts naturally found around grapes, it would have been almost impossible to prevent the start of spontaneous fermentation. Storing grapes or grape juice for any period of time meant that you ended up with a rudimentary wine whether you wanted it or not.

The transportation of wine has historically been a significant issue. As a liquid, its weight and the need for watertight containers made distribution difficult and costly. These factors influenced the way that wine was shipped and the geographic scope of the wine trade. The slow pace of travel and trade meant that the wine containers could be exposed to the elements for long periods. This, in combination with continuous fermentation, meant that the wine reaching its destination might be significantly different from the wine that was originally shipped. Wine was a valuable commodity, but it was not always easy to obtain it in adequate quantities, at affordable prices, or of appropriate quality. As such, having wine often necessitated having the grapes and an ability to grow them locally.

An important influence on the early wine trade and the diffusion of grapes was their use in the practices and ceremonies of different religions. Religious practice required that wine be available. This complemented the existing consumer markets for wine. Wine and grape plants moved along trade routes and with religious missionaries. There was not a common worldwide market for wine as we see today. Wine was traded in very limited circles. Local variations in climate, grapes, winemaking processes, and tastes meant that the quality of wine varied considerably from place to place and from trade route to trade route.

While religion played a role in the diffusion of wine, it may not have been a starring role. The spread of wine production through trade and colonialism would likely have been far more important. To see how this evolves we can begin by looking at the ancient trading cultures of the Mediterranean, the Greeks, in particular. They, as well as the Phoenicians and other trading peoples of the Mediterranean basin, changed the geography of wine and the wine trade. They traded wine and grapes across the Mediterranean. In doing so they began the transformation of the wine trade as well as wine's link to political geography. This is one case where the notion that all of western culture begins with the Greeks actually has some validity.

The mercantile cultures of the classical Greek world did not begin the wine trade. Their political evolution did, however, significantly influence the trade in wine. The transition from small city-states to commercial empires created opportunities for trading wine and the diffusion of grapevines. For those unfamiliar with the concept, a city-state (Singapore is a modern-day example) is an extremely small country, consisting of a city and its immediate surroundings. City-states have a very limited territory from which to draw resources. Today, city-states such as Monaco, Andorra, and others draw resources from neighboring countries, if not the rest of the world. The classical world was much different. A country's wealth was in large part tied to the resources of its lands. The smaller the country, the more limited were its potential resources.

In large countries trade is often internal. With small countries trade is, by necessity, external, and external trade brings with it politics. In the political environment of the classical Greek world, city-states were often in conflict. Countries that were already limited in resources because of their size were forced to use up what limited resources they had for defensive purposes. Fortifications and a large military came at the cost of consumer spending. This would have limited the amount of money available to support trade and would have made local wine production important.

As the city-states grew and consolidated, resources previously spent on protection from their neighbors could be turned to other applications. The Mediterranean, Aegean, Adriatic, and Black seas became trading routes for expanding mercantile empires. Trading colonies around those seas gave the Greeks the ability to trade their products and spread their culture. Because wine and grapes were part of their culture and profitable commodities, they traveled along with the Greek traders, who influenced the diffusion of wine and established patterns of commerce that exist to this day.

In spite of its history, most consumers are unfamiliar with Greek wine. Your local wine store may not even carry them. Our lack of familiarity with Greek wine is a product of the last thousand years or so and should in no way be seen as a reflection on the importance of classical Greece to the geography of wine. It is the result of the Greeks being overshadowed by the Romans and is a product of the Great Schism and the Crusades. It is also because of the fall of Byzantium and the Ottoman Turk conquest. These served to isolate the eastern Mediterranean from the growing global wine market. Greek winemaking became internalized, its production aimed at local consumers. This is changing as Greek vintners reach out to the world market. Some vintners are switching to more common grape varietals. Labeling is also being modified so that foreign consumers can read the labels without understanding the Cyrillic alphabet. More adventurous wine consumers are also trying traditional Greek wines. Even so, the limited exposure to Greek wines may lead some to question their contributions to wine and its geography. They shouldn't.

THE ROMAN DIFFUSION OF WINE

The Greeks laid the foundation for the wine industry that we know today. The Romans picked up where the Greeks left off and made it into a vital part of their economy. Just as the Greeks brought wine with them as they traded across the Mediterranean, so did the Romans as they conquered most of the known world of their day.

The Italian peninsula was the political and economic core of an extensive military and economic empire. It was also the center of wine production and a major consumer of wine produced in other parts of the empire. As with the Greeks before them, the Romans traded wine around the Mediterranean basin. The Mediterranean was a highway for the transport of wine and other products, and the Italian peninsula was at the center of that highway.

The geographic importance of the Roman Empire was that it created an environment under which trade could flourish. Areas of conflict were on the fringes of the empire. Away from those areas of conflict the empire was secure and well regulated. Military spending was still high, but the resources of the empire allowed for significant public expenditures on other things. Tax revenues paid for the development of extensive road systems and ports that facilitated trade, helping to create more wealth. More wealth meant more money to spend on consumer goods, including wine. Moreover, wine was subject to taxation, and thus important to the health of the Roman economy. As a consequence we see in the Romans some of the first governmental efforts to control and regulate the crop, precursors of modern-day agricultural regulation.

The power of the empire meant the spread of Roman culture. This was important for wine. Wine was more than just another consumer good for the Romans. It was part of their culture. For both financial and cultural reasons, wine followed in the wake of the legions.

The geography of the Roman conquests had a significant impact on the evolution of wine. The growth of the empire took the Romans to areas outside the Mediterranean basin and to regions with climates that were very different from those of the Italian peninsula. This was a problem for vintners using varietals that were adapted to the conditions of the Italian peninsula. For a culture that prized wine, the problem needed to be solved. It could be solved with nonwine alcohols, or it could be solved by importing wine from elsewhere in the empire. The solutions to the problem of climate could also be solved by working with indigenous grapes and by working with the grapes from home that survived the more hostile conditions. This would have been a far cry from modern selective-breeding programs but we can look at these activities as the first steps toward the development of many of the wine grape varietals that we know today.

The fall of the Roman Empire had a significant impact on the diffusion of wine and the wine trade. The Dark Ages and feudalism limited trade and isolated many of the wine-producing regions. As we shall see, urbanization in Europe eventually changed the geography of the wine trade. It was not, however, until the Renaissance and the Age of Exploration that wine begins to diffuse beyond the bounds of Europe. This diffusion is tied to the end of feudalism, the rebirth of empires, and the extension of their power across the oceans.

WINE AND POLITICAL GEOGRAPHY

As we begin to see with the Greeks and Romans, the geography of wine has a lot to do with political geography and colonization. Whenever there are a limited number of producers who can control a valuable commodity market, the potential is there for some interesting trading relationships. This has definitely been true with wine. Major wine consumers routinely found themselves in uneasy trade relationships in which they were purchasing wine from unreliable political allies or even from their political adversaries. As in any import relationship where there is a highly sought-after product and a limited number of producers, the exporters had the freedom to dictate prices on whatever terms they saw fit. A modern analogy is the relationship between

OPEC and the major oil importers of the world. Whether it was the wine trade of centuries past or the oil trade of today, great powers do not appreciate being at risk to trade embargoes, price gouging, or the political whims of their trading partners.

Using the example of OPEC, we can argue that the economic influence of oil forces countries to treat the OPEC nations a bit differently. Having a resource that somebody desperately wants gives you a certain degree of power. Admittedly, political history has never been governed by wine, but changing alliances and military conflicts have influenced the wine trade. New allies meant new sources of wine. Political conflicts produced wine embargoes, higher wine tariffs, and price gouging. What set early power politics apart from what we are used to today was that it included colonialism: the political, military, and economic subjugation of a place and its people by another nation and its people. It is motivated by the economic, military, and/or political interests of the colonizing power(s). For four hundred years, the major European powers gobbled up as much territory as they could. In doing so they competed with their neighbors and tried to capitalize on all of the resource opportunities that their new lands presented.

Wine has, in some cases quite literally, been caught in the crossfire of international power relationships. Although wine has never been the direct cause of colonialism, colonialism's impact on wine has been substantial. Colonialism expanded wine production across the globe. Although the diffusion of wine was simply a by-product of colonialism, the modern map of wine production is a direct result of more than five hundred years of colonialism.

Before we look at any examples of colonialism and its impact on the wine industry, it is important that we lay a good foundation of understanding. While the details of colonial expansion and conquest can be quite complex, where they relate to wine they are rather simple, and depend on whether or not the colonizing power was a wine producer.

The colonizing population always carries with it the trappings of home, and those powers that were wine producers transported viticulture and wine abroad into the colonized territory. As a staple of their daily lives, it was an important part of their identity, and having wine and grapes helped the colonizers to feel at home in their new environments. Colonists brought their language, food, architecture, and tangible goods that reminded them of home. Today, many of these trappings of colonial life are still readily visible. We can see them in the places, the architecture, the language, and the culture of the people.

In colonies of wine-producing nations, obtaining that wine from home was not always easy or economically feasible. As a result, wine production in the colonies was driven by necessity or simply by the high cost of importing wine from the home country. Satisfying local demand for wine also gave individuals in the colony—at least those with experience in growing grapes and making wine—a potentially lucrative cash crop. If there was any way possible to produce grapes, you could be sure that the colonists would find it.

This, of course, assumes that colonists were allowed to grow grapes. After all, part of the purpose of a colony is to make money for the people at home. A self-sufficient colony was counterproductive because it cut down on profitability. Colonists who grow grapes and make wine for themselves do not buy high-priced wine from the mother country. Even worse, colonists may prove to be so good at growing grapes and producing wine that they might want to *sell* wine to the home country. This was usually not the case, but if the environment was right it was a possibility.

Viticulture was considered profitable, so for colonial powers that were not wine producers themselves, colonialism was a means of gaining access to lands with growing conditions suitable for viticulture. Only limitations of climate explains why the English and Dutch, who consumed great amounts of wine, were not themselves wine producers. Being significant wine consumers but negligible wine producers made them the greatest wine importers of their day. Consequently, they had an ongoing interest in establishing colonies capable of exporting wine back to the mother country. They never quite succeeded in their efforts, but they sure did try.

As a consequence of colonialism, viticulture and wine production diffused across the globe. It was, in a sense, a great geographic experiment. Colonists from home countries that were wine producers tried to make wine wherever they went. At the same time, entrepreneurs from non–wine-producing countries scoured their colonies to find the one place where they could make a killing in the wine trade. Along the way there were some tremendous success stories, the evidence of which is still visible today in wine stores, as well as some abysmal failures that have been lost to the history books.

COLONIAL POWERS AND WINE

The saying that the sun never set on the British Empire was testament to their success at colonialism. At the height of the

British Empire, its colonial holdings were so vast that it was always daytime somewhere in the empire. While the British may have ruled a tremendous amount of the earth's surface, one thing they never accomplished was to eliminate their reliance on imported wine. Consider the wine map of today and how it relates to British colonialism of the past. South Africa, Australia, and New Zealand are major wine producers, but wine production in these countries has only recently become competitive in the world market. They were the only significant British colonies climatically capable of producing large amounts of wine. However, they were not economically viable sources for supplying the demand for wine at home. Even if they were capable of producing enough wine to satisfy Victorian-era British demand for wine, the cost of getting the wine to market would have been exorbitant. A map will immediately tell us that European wine-producing countries were a heck of a lot closer. Assuming that Britain was not at war with them, it would be much cheaper to obtain wine from Europe rather than from faraway colonies.

The benefits and liabilities of seeking wine supplies closer to home is best illustrated by the ongoing relationship between the British and Portuguese. Spain annexed Portugal in 1580. At that time, Britain and Spain were at odds, so trade between the two nations suffered. British entrepreneurs started to work their way into Portugal and the wine trade expanded. Then the Portuguese had the bad judgment to side with Charles I in the English civil war. Charles lost—he was beheaded—and Portuguese wine trade took a big hit. Britain went to war with France in 1678. By then Britain had forgiven the Portuguese, so wine exports increased. The Portuguese benefited even more when they allied themselves with the English and Dutch in 1703. The Napoleonic wars and French occupation temporarily cut off Portuguese exports to Britain until Portugal was occupied by the British. By the 1850s the British were turning away from port in favor of sherry due to the high prices of port and improved relations with Spain. This play-by-play of almost four hundred years of British and Portuguese history is terribly limited, but it underscores how the intricacies of European history could affect the patterns of trade in commodities such as wine.

SOUTH AFRICA AND CHILE

To the European superpowers of the eighteenth and nineteenth centuries, South Africa was a key strategic location. It possessed natural seaports, especially Cape Town, from which naval power could control trade going around the Cape of Good Hope into the Indian Ocean. This led the Dutch to colonize the cape, hence the establishment of the Dutch Cape Colony. The Dutch were soon followed by the British, who extended their colonial holdings from the coastline into the resource-rich lands of the interior.

The conditions of soil and climate near Cape Town approximate those in southern France. Warm weather combined with the moderating influence of the Atlantic and protection from the drying winds of the interior made it an obvious place to try wine production. Today, the region is home to high-quality producers of European grape cultivars. The Dutch and later the

British colonizers were not, however, well versed in producing wine, so the history of South African wine production makes for an interesting geographic study. Much like Madeira, the early Cape Colony wine producers did have some advantage in their location. European vessels sailing around the cape would have already been at sea for a long time. The cape ports thus made a logical stop for water and other supplies, including wine. The advantage to wine producers was that they could sell almost anything to the passing ships. Where else were they going to go? No matter what their wine was like, somebody would probably buy it. Selling wine of dubious quality was not exactly what the Dutch, and later the British, had in mind. They were hoping to make money in the wine trade and looking for an alternative to imports from the French.

Here is where cultural geography becomes relevant to the discussion of colonialism. When we talk about migration in geography we talk about the movement of people. We also talk about what those people bring with them. When the Dutch and the British arrived in present-day South Africa, they brought with them their culture and their language, their economic systems and technical knowledge. What they did not bring was much wine expertise. This was not because they had no interest in it. On the contrary, as a potential moneymaker they were very interested. But the climate of the Cape Colony was very different from that of England or Holland, countries with cool marine climates where water was considered to be an unlimited resource. The Cape Colony, its arid climate, and an unfamiliar crop would have been a real challenge. Today, they have overcome these challenges, but it took a long time.

A century or so before the British came to rule the waves the world's great colonial power was Spain. Spain's New World colonies were a tremendous source of wealth. As a means of securing that wealth and organizing their colonial holdings, the Spanish did things quite literally by the book in their "Laws of the Indes." The folks back home wanted to ensure that they got their share of the New World's wealth, and as they were just emerging from generations of warfare against the Moors, they needed the money. They also needed to keep a tight rein on the ambitious men that they had dispatched to conquer these new lands. Once lands and peoples were conquered, viable colonies needed to be secured and the locals needed to be converted to Christianity. The Spanish were very methodical in their approach to colonization.

Spanish colonization of much of the western hemisphere transported wine production to the New World. The Spanish were wine producers and it was a part of their diet. They were Catholic and it was part of their religious practice. The problem was that the colonies were a long distance from the wine sources in Spain. The length of time to get to and from Spain and the expense of transportation provided incentives for producing wine in the colonies. Unfortunately, many of Spain's new territories were in climates that were less than ideal for wine production.

The tropical climates of most of Spain's colonies should have created a lucrative market for the regions that could support wine production. Climate should have created networks of trade between the colonies. The fact that it did not was due to the way in which the Spanish regulated trade. In the Spanish system trade was centered on the home country, so the trade of wine within the region was limited. Even after independence, the wine-producing regions served primarily local markets. The importance of this can be seen in the rather slow emergence of Spain's former colonies onto the international wine market.

In the western hemisphere there are a number of former Spanish colonies whose climates have potential for significant wine production, primarily Chile and Argentina. There are also regions in the other Andean countries as well as in Mexico, with climates suitable for wine production. Wine production is growing in Argentina, but it and the other former Spanish colonies still produce wine largely for local consumption.

Of these colonies, only Chile is a significant producer of wine for world export. As geographers we are very interested not only in the connections that exist between places, but also in what happens in isolated regions. There are many reasons a region or a country might be isolated, and we are interested both in the reasons as well as in the effect of the isolation. Because Chile has long been geographically and politically isolated from the world wine market, it is an especially interesting object of study as a product of the colonial diffusion of wine and as an isolated wine producer.

Stretching along the southwestern coast of South America, Chile presented Spanish colonists with a variety of climate conditions from which to choose. In the far north, the easterly winds passing over the Andes results in a strong rain shadow effect. It is there that we find the Atacama Desert, one of the driest environments on Earth. At the southern tip of the country, Patagonia boasts a climate that is as cold and inhospitable as anywhere in South America. In the approximate center of the country is Chile's capital, Santiago. In the valleys both north and south of Santiago the cold coastal ocean currents, westerly winds, coastal mountain ranges, and inland valleys produce conditions similar to those of northern California. And as in California, the valleys surrounding Santiago, as well as on the eastern side of the Andes in the Mendoza province of Argentina, have become significant producers of wine.

The production of wine locally would have been important to the colonizing Spanish because Chile was about as isolated as one can get from wine sources in Spain and the wine markets elsewhere in Europe. Just to get to Buenos Aires from Valparaiso, Santiago's port city, requires a sail of nearly 2,000 miles. Moreover, it requires sailing through the treacherous waters of Cape Horn at the southern tip of the continent. The distance involved in shipping wine from Spain, and the high resulting costs and limited availability, would have put a premium on local wine and the knowledge of how to produce it.

The physical distance and isolation of Chile from the wine regions of Europe and North America did have one advantage for the country's wine producers. It helped to isolate them from the biotic threats that decimated the wineries of Europe and North America. Phylloxera never reached Chile. Neither did powdery mildew. Unfortunately, the physical isolation that spared Chile from these hazards also prevented Chilean wine producers from capitalizing on them. Even though Chile was independent of Spanish rule as of 1810, its wine producers still had to face the economic reality of its geographic isolation. Separated from major markets, wine production in Chile developed to satisfy local needs and tastes. This is typical of commodity production in isolated regions.

In the story of wine and political geography, Chile and South Africa have a great deal in common. Colonialism brought wine production while physical isolation suppressed its development. Until 1990 the two countries also shared in a sort of sociopolitical isolation from wine consumers in Europe and North America. In 1990, General Augusto Pinochet was voted out of office as president of Chile. He achieved the presidency in a coup d'état that toppled the Marxist presidency of Salvador Allende and which resulted in the deaths of thousands of dissidents and in the torture of tens of thousands of others. Also in 1990, South African president F. W. de Klerk ordered the release of Nelson Mandela from prison and began the process that formally ended apartheid in 1994. With these changes, the wines of Chile and South Africa gained a level of social acceptance that was previously lacking.

Social acceptance, foreign investment, familiar varietals, and improvements in quality have allowed Chilean and South African wines to reach beyond their local markets. This has also been made possible by improvements in transportation that have dramatically reduced the time and cost of getting their wines to market. Thanks to the relatively low cost of labor in Chile and South Africa, they can undersell most of their wine rivals. While Chile and South Africa may not have the reputation of other wine-producing countries, the variety of wines they export and their relatively low cost give their producers a marketing edge that enables them to reach out to international wine consumers and to introduce them to what their wines have to offer.

Chapter 11

URBANIZATION AND THE
WINE GEOGRAPHY

The growth of the wine industry into what exists today is in large part a product of urbanization and the industrial revolution. Colonialism took wine to the far corners of the earth, but urbanization truly changed it into an industry. Urbanization and the Industrial Revolution fundamentally altered how we live, where we live, and what we do for a living. In terms of wine and the wine industry, they took wine from the domain of gardening and local bartering to an industrial concern and an object of global trade.

Although wine predates the first cities, urbanization helped to create the modern wine industry. The growth of cities created a population that wanted wine but was incapable of producing it. People living in cities were disconnected from the land as well as from food and beverage production. Urbanization created a society of wine consumers, and so wine producers were able to take advantage of industrial advances, transportation improvements, and a growing body of scientific knowledge to increase production and feed the urban demand for wine.

URBANIZATION AND THE WINE TRADE

There are significant environmental limitations to where grapes can be grown and wine produced. In an agricultural region that cannot produce grapes, individuals can satisfy their desire for alcohol through production of something other than wine (beer, hard cider, or spirits). However, there may still be consumers out there who really like wine. The problem is how to get that wine to a small number of isolated consumers and still make a profit. In medieval Europe the answer was fairs.

Today we think of fairs as a place to take the kids so that they can see farm animals, eat lots of fried food, and ride on unsafe-looking machinery. It is about entertainment. A few hundred years ago fairs were more like markets. They were about trade. Once a year merchants and tradesmen would come to sell their wares and supply the local population with items that were not produced locally. This included the sale of wine. Unfortunately this format was not conducive to selling large amounts of wine, since consumers would have had to buy a year's supply all at once. Given the poor state of transportation, even getting the wine to the fairs was a difficult challenge to overcome.

As populations grow, fairs can become more frequent. Seasonal fairs can evolve into weekly market days. If the population grows large enough the weekly markets evolve into permanent commercial establishments. This evolution has a dramatic impact on the cost of transportation and the profit margins for traders. Rather than having to travel to hamlets and villages all over the region, traders can go to a single city. The traders do not go to the people in the countryside. The people come to the city.

For traders this meant that they could save on costs by transporting their product to just one spot. It becomes economically feasible to bring shipments in more often. So if we are talking about wine, then population growth allows us to evolve from seasonal purchases at fairs to daily purchases from traders in the city.

It is important to remember that not all villages grew into cities. The ones that did tended to be in locations that had a little something extra such as good transportation access. Better access simplified trade and increased potential profits. The net result was the development of a permanent trading infrastructure of marketplaces, warehousing, and guildhalls as well as the growth of a sizable population of traders and financiers. This is true not just for wine, but for other trade goods as well.

Population growth and urbanization had an additional benefit for the wine trade. In the city, the population is not capable of producing their own alcohol. So they have to buy whatever they drink. There would be more consumers and more profit potential for those producers who could get their product to market. As the population was going to have to buy alcohol anyway, there was the possibility that they would buy something other than the local brew. They might buy more wine.

If we project the process over an entire society with many new cities, the impact is magnified. Trade becomes an issue of national concern where a great deal of money is at stake. It becomes an issue of treaties and a cause of conflict. As technology improves it is applied to make trade easier and more profitable. Canals and railroads become rational investments to facilitate trade and to generate wealth. The effects of urbanization thus expand to affect entire economies.

This takes us back to those regions that would be exporting wine to the aforementioned urban marketplaces. We begin with pre-urbanization. There are a myriad of small producers who live in villages and supply themselves and a limited number of local establishments. Outside demand provides a potential for profit that some producers can exploit. This provides them with the capital necessary to increase their production. Given enough time, small producers trading locally give way to large producers whose primary market is for export.

The desire to export wine does not, however, translate into the ability to export wine. Individual producers, even large ones, may not produce enough wine on their own to make export economically feasible. Without a ship to transport wine, and without a facility to store wine or a means of getting it to the storage facility, even those who can produce large quantities of wine will not be able to export it. Building a port and a trading infrastructure requires many people and a great deal of investment. In cities, the necessary resources and facilities would be available. By building on economies of scale (the economic benefits of large-scale facilities/production) cities could offer wine producers significant trading advantages. Advantages for trade mean more profits for producers. In so doing, cities become the export points for networks of wine producers and the home for merchants, financiers, and transporters linked to those networks.

BURGUNDY

Many wine regions in Europe flourished as the continent became more and more urbanized. Burgundy is a compelling case study because unlike Bordeaux and Oporto, two success stories of the link between the wine trade and urbanization, Burgundy became successful *in spite of* its isolation from France's growing urban centers.

Burgundy is less than two hundred miles from Paris, which is and has for centuries been the largest city in France. If winemakers could produce a good product and get that product to Paris, they could make a lucrative profit, so access to the Parisian wine market was very important. For winemakers in Burgundy who did not want to ship their product to Paris, the city of Lyon, with its growing textile industry, was a hundred miles to the south. So why was Burgundy isolated from urban wine markets? What we need to keep in mind is that up until the mid-1800s water was still the primary means of transporting goods to market. This was important for Burgundy, as its water-based trade was to the south, via the Rhône River and its tributaries. Although Burgundy may be geographically close to Paris, its transportation network was oriented toward the south. Any wine to be shipped from Burgundy to Paris had to travel over land until it could be loaded onto barges that could then be floated down the Seine to Paris. The cost of land-based transportation and the ability of ships to carry larger loads was the impetus for canal building, including the construction of the Burgundy Canal. Prior to the construction of the canal, wine shipped from Burgundy would have been more expensive than that of its competitors due to the cost of the overland shipment.

In terms of the Parisian wine market, Chablis, Champagne, and the Loire supplied the vast majority of the wine consumed. Once again, geography plays a key role. Chablis and Champagne are obvious, as they are located on tributaries of the Seine; their wine could be loaded on barges and shipped directly downstream into the very heart of the city. The Loire was a bit more complex. It was not linked by river to Paris. Loire producers were able to eventually reach Paris through the construction of the Briare Canal. The Briare was a technologically straightforward canal built through relatively flat terrain. It was also a vital link between the productive farmlands of the Loire and Paris consumers. The ease of construction and the importance of the project enabled the Briare Canal to be completed in the seventeenth century. The link between Burgundy and Paris was accomplished with the completion of the Burgundy Canal. Unlike the Briare Canal, the Burgundy Canal was a technologically complex and expensive canal to build, and was not completed until almost two hundred years later. Access to Paris via the Briare Canal meant that the Loire vintners could get tremendous amounts of wine to a market that was growing by leaps and bounds. Burgundy had to find a different approach.

The alternative for Burgundy wine merchants could have been Lyon. River access would have made shipping their products downstream to Lyon a rather simple matter. In southern Burgundy (Mâcon and Beaujolais) that was indeed a viable option, given their proximity to Lyon. For most Burgundy producers, especially in the Côte d'Or, the small size of Lyon and the extent of the competition meant that Paris was still a more appealing target for their wine.

What did Burgundian winemakers who had a problem reaching the big city do to sell their products? They had to either find a new market or a new way of getting the product there, and finding a new market was not an option. Getting the product to market was accomplished through the completion of the Burgundy Canal, but what did they do before 1822, when no alternate market and no transportation alternative were available? With their only options being to get out of the business or change their product to facilitate transport, they developed a new marketing strategy that is still in place to this day: They went "upmarket."

In the mass market, price is a dominant factor in the ability of producers to sell their products. For producers with high transportation costs this is a significant problem. How does one compete when transportation costs are much higher than for the competition? If competition on the mass market is not practical, some producers can go upmarket. That is, they produce a smaller amount of a higher-value product. This has two benefits. First, it is easier to transport as there is less volume/weight to ship. Second, by creating a product of higher quality, producers can market to consumers who are more quality and less cost conscious. Selling less is offset by selling at a higher price. In the world of wine this means that we do not compete with other producers for the mass market. What we do is invest our time, energy, and money into high-end production. We ship smaller amounts of more valuable wine aimed at the more affluent consumer. The cost of transportation is carried with the product to a clientele that is less cost conscious. This is how Burgundian wine producers overcame their isolation and were able to reach urban markets.

Burgundy is a great place to study the geography of wine, because there are few places that provide so many variations in the kind of wine produced and in the environments in which it is produced. Part of the diversity of Burgundy is that it really is not just one wine-producing region. The focus of Burgundy wine is the thin strip of land known as the Côte d'Or. But Burgundy also includes Chablis to the north, as well as the Côte Chalonnaise, the Mâconnais, and the Beaujolais regions to the south. Each region is different from the other and together they lend variety to the wines that come out of Burgundy.

The Côte d'Or, Chablis, Mâconnais, and Beaujolais are similar in the fact that they are grape monocultures. In those areas where the soil is suitable for wine production, vineyards predominate. Even so, these regions look different. In the Côte d'Or you will find pinot noir production, along with a little chardonnay, along a single southeast-facing ridgeline. In Chablis the dominant grape is chardonnay, which is produced on a series of mainly south-facing hillsides. In both cases you can see the influence of microclimate and geology in the location of the vineyards. In Mâconnais it is also chardonnay, but the vineyards tend to be on the high ground and are punctuated by many small villages. In Beaujolais, the gamay grape is staked out (not trellised) everywhere. The Côte Chalonnaise is an anomaly because it is a region of mixed farming and lacks a grape monoculture. It is, however, a very pretty place if you are a fan of agricultural landscapes.

What also sets the regions of Burgundy apart is their history. Chablis is on tributaries of the Seine, which afforded the region easy access to the markets of Paris. Beaujolais is on tributaries of the Rhône, which gave it access to the markets of Lyon. Without easy river access to major urban markets, the Côte d'Or could not directly compete with its neighbors due to the cost of overland shipment. It simply cost more to get their wine to market. Rather than invest in high volume and low cost, the

Côte d'Or went in the direction of low volume, high quality, and high cost. The high quality would attract consumers who were willing to pay the higher costs, which led to the development of Burgundy's reputation for high-quality (and higher-priced) wines that it carries to this day.

If we compare Burgundy with the other preeminent French wine region of Bordeaux, we will find that there is much more to the wine landscape of Burgundy than just geology and rivers. Bordeaux is a region known for its big producers and châteaux vineyards. When we buy Bordeaux we are buying wines that are produced in the same châteaux vineyards where the grapes are grown. In Burgundy this is not the case. In Burgundy the vineyards are much smaller. This is partly because the climate and geology limit the area available for vineyards and partly the result of the redistribution of lands after the French Revolution. Given the limited size of the vineyards and the costs of wine production, it made economic sense for wine production to be separated from the growing of wine grapes. The vineyards are associated with specialized winemakers (or *negociants*) like Louis Jadot and Louis Latour who purchase from the vintners within the region. Rather than having large châteaux vineyards as in Bordeaux, Burgundy has many small vineyards that sell their grapes to producers in the towns. Visually, this arrangement gives Burgundy a more traditional rural appearance, which draws tourists to the region's small towns where the wines are produced.

The Problem with Urbanization Today

The urbanization of Europe established a new geography of trade in wine. Unfortunately the pattern of urbanization has changed over time. Two hundred years ago, cities were dense and compact. The areas of even the largest cities were small enough to be walkable. That was before the automobile and commuter railroads. Today, cities are huge sprawling places. Even where urban populations are stable, cities are rapidly sprawling outward. The problem for fans of good wine is that the growth of cities can come at the expense of agricultural and viticultural lands.

With urban sprawl, cities rapidly chew up agricultural land. Large farms or vineyards offer developers an opportunity to build big and profit big. Agricultural lands tend to be flat, well drained, and easy to redevelop for housing, retail, and other urban land use. It is also much cheaper and easier for developers to build on large tracts of land than to buy up many small parcels for development. As this process continues it raises the value of surrounding properties, eventually leading to their development. Even if the current generation of farmers (or vintners) does not want to sell, the increasing value of their land means that their children might have to sell off the land to pay the capital gains and/or inheritance taxes. As a result, the amount of prime farmland dwindles.

Even if vineyards remain in operation, the costs of sprawl are significant. Urban and suburban residents may object to the use of fertilizers and pesticides, smells from plant and animal wastes, and noise associated with agricultural machinery on neighboring farms. Likewise, even if a vineyard is on good terms with its neighbors, sprawl detracts from the visual appeal of wine landscapes. A vineyard in a natural setting may be attractive and have romantic appeal. This image cannot help but suffer when that very same vineyard is surrounded by tract housing, fast-food restaurants, and motels.

The impact of sprawl on wine production is not yet a factor in Burgundy, but it is a factor in the areas close to the city of Bordeaux. In Europe, local government has a great deal of control over how land is used. In the United States those controls are much weaker. As a consequence, sprawl is a significant threat to viticulture in areas near rapidly growing metropolitan areas such as those in Northern California. The same urban development that once fueled the evolution of the wine industry is now a threat to the health of that industry.

Chapter 12

ECONOMIC GEOGRAPHY AND WINE

$\mathscr{If}$ you are like me, you have probably purchased wine in different types of retail environments. Although I have my favorite stores, many of the wines I buy can be found in almost any store that sells wine—local liquor stores, grocery stores, or "big box" bulk food providers—though I may not admit to it at a party when I am feverishly uncorking bottles and scratching off price tags.

It can seem as though there is little rhyme or reason to it, but in reality there is a reason and a pattern to what is sold and especially where it is sold. Both factors are important to the profitability of a business. As long as business has profit as a goal, geography will be an important consideration. It is like the Seurat painting discussed in an earlier chapter. Up close all we see are meaningless dots. If we step back and look at the painting from a broader perspective, those dots form recognizable patterns. That is what the geography of retail is like. We are just used to having our noses pressed up against the glass.

Retail geography is a subset of economic geography. Unlike other types of economic geography, retail geography is something with which we are very familiar. As a reader of this book you have undoubtedly purchased wine before. You have been to a liquor store and may have visited a winery, and have thus experienced retail geography firsthand. We just need to take a few steps back in order to see and understand the pattern of who sells wine, where they sell it, and what they sell.

The first step in the process of understanding wine retailing and its geography is to do a bit of translation by thinking of profit and loss not just as dollar amounts. When we look at a retail operation we can identify a dollar figure at which the operation will break even. We call this its threshold. From that dollar figure we can make the jump to talking about customers. In doing so our threshold evolves from a monetary unit to a number of customers. The threshold for a wine shop translates into the number of paying customers it must attract to break even.

To determine the geography of profit and loss for a wine store we need one more piece of information. We must identify the store's market area. Market area is the area in which the shop is the cheapest buying location. Though there are sometimes exceptions, the assumption here is that we will patronize the establishment that offers what we want at the best price. Assuming that we act in an economically rational manner, we can then identify the market area of our favorite wine store. We can compare prices with its competitors, look at travel costs for customers getting to the store, and we can come up with a pretty good approximation as to where the customers are. Here is where we can make the leap to profit-and-loss calculations. Does the market area contain enough regular wine purchasers to keep the store in business? Is the threshold population of customers within the market area? If there are more customers in the market area than are needed to break even, then we have geographically defined profit. If there are too few customers in the market area, we have loss.

In addition to thinking about profit and loss geographically, we can also look at the goods being sold and how they influence purchase patterns. We classify goods as being convenience goods or shopping goods. Shopping goods are those that we shop for the best price and highest quality. These are goods where there is a great deal of difference between producers and/or models and where costs are high, such as cars and major appliances. Convenience goods are those where costs tend to be low, that are purchased often, with little or no difference between producers, and where immediate access is the key to purchases. Milk is a good example of a convenience good. We will travel long distances to purchase shopping goods. There may be major price differences between retailers. There may be differences in the level of service provided. Not all local retailers may have what we want. (If we really want a Mercedes, a Toyota will not do.) Convenience goods we buy as close to home as possible. Why travel farther than the corner store for a gallon of milk?

Wine throws us a curve ball in that it is both a convenience good and a shopping good. Some wines we will travel long distances to buy. They are expensive and differ markedly from producer to producer, as well as from year to year. Other wines are inexpensive and offer little variation. We can go to the closest store that sells wine and buy what we need. The dividing line between wines that are convenience goods and wines that are shopping goods is not exact. It varies from one consumer to the next.

With this understanding we can look at individual wine retailers and begin to make sense of their approach to selling wine. Consider the examples of a specialist wine store that sells high-end wines, the neighborhood liquor store, and a grocery store that sells wine. The specialist wine store sells wine as a shopping good. It carries wines that other providers will not stock. It may also stock the normal assortment of table wines, beers, and liquors. Someone who wants more than the run-of-the-mill wine may bypass a wide variety of other providers to shop at the specialist store. Quality service, experienced staff, wine tastings, and other activities can increase the profile and attractiveness of the store. Prices may be higher at the specialist store, but they make up for it by drawing in customers from a much wider area. Given their approach to selling wine, their market area will overlap that of neighborhood liquor stores.

The neighborhood liquor store sells wine as a convenience good. It does not specialize in wine. Instead, it offers an assortment of alcohols that move off the shelf very quickly. If we need a bottle of wine and are not picky, the neighborhood liquor store will meet our needs. Our choice of whites may be limited to American chardonnay, but if that is all that we need there's no need to travel any farther. The neighborhood liquor store may have a very small market area, but if there are a high number of customers in that area, the business can be quite successful.

Somewhere in between the high-end wine stores and the neighborhood liquor stores is the grocery store. In states that allow grocery stores to sell wine, the stores stock wines primarily as convenience goods. However, they outcompete the neighborhood liquor store by also stocking some higher-end wines. They will not rival the specialist wine shops for selection or service. The grocery store strategy is price and ease of purchase. The grocery store sells enough other things that it can afford to mark down the cost of the wine. As chain groceries buy in bulk, they may also be able to leverage deals with wine distributors that allow them to undersell their competitors. Even if the prices are identical, the ease of picking up a bottle of wine in the process of doing the rest of the shopping gives the grocery store a competitive advantage. By virtue of its chosen strategy, the grocery store will dominate the middle of the wine market. As there are a limited number of wine customers in an area, and as the middle is where most of the customers are, it makes life very difficult for those at the high or low ends of the market.

The effect of a major retailer in the local wine market is significant. With enough of a pure convenience market, the neighborhood liquor stores may be able to survive and profitably sell wine. With enough customers in the area to support a specialist wine shop, it too may coexist with a grocery store. It is almost impossible, however, to beat the grocery store at its own game. As a result, the grocery store may end up being the only local wine provider in smaller towns and villages. This is an approach that has proven itself to be amazingly successful not just for wine sales but for retailing as a whole. It is the "big box" style of retailing that many associate in a negative light.

Wine, Central Place Theory, and the Internet

In reality, wine retailers come in all shapes and sizes. Understanding their geography requires a fair amount of local knowledge. Understanding the theory behind it comes down to a few geographic basics. People will, in general, travel to the closest buying location that has what they want. Price can influence that pattern by making certain buying locations more attractive than others. Large populations will support more sales. Larger populations will also allow for greater specialization in the products being sold. If a town has too few people for local retailers to offer a product, consumers will have to travel to bigger towns to find what they need.

The retail geography basics outlined above are true for wine as well as for other kinds of products and services. This link between population, communities, and the availability of products/services is at the heart of Central Place Theory (CPT). The theory seeks to explain the pattern of communities over the landscape based on issues of population and retail/service provision. CPT stems from the work of Walter Christaller, who studied these linkages in northern Germany during the late 1920s. His research has been applied repeatedly in places that, like northern Germany, are flat and have a fairly even distribution of population. In those kinds of environments the even spread of population and the lack of landscape variations results in a very organized pattern of communities.

While CPT works best for studying the pattern of towns in the Great Plains, it can also be applied to wine retailing. Imagine a local map. The smallest villages and towns on it may have a single retailer that offers only basic wines. They do not have a population capable of supporting anything more than that. The larger towns on the map may have enough people to support multiple retailers and maybe even some specialized retailers. These towns will be the destination for people who could not find the wines that they wanted in the small towns. This is Central Place Theory as applied to wine. It does not always work perfectly. If you live in a little town that just happens to have a big and well-stocked wine store, consider yourself one of the lucky exceptions to the rule.

When looking at how and where we buy wine it is important to recognize that we are talking about the modern world of retailing. That world has evolved through some incredible periods of change. Just consider how the wine market and how we purchase wine has evolved over the last thirty years. If we look back over a few hundred years of retail history, the changes have been enormous.

Of all the changes that have taken place the most significant from a geographic perspective is Internet retailing. Distance is an important concept in geography. With travel and transportation costs, the greater the distance between you and someplace else, the less you are likely to go to—or even know about—that place. Overcoming the "friction" of distance is integral to many of our most basic geographical models of human behavior. Some argue that the Internet makes geography less important by eliminating the "friction of distance." Others argue that the Internet makes geography more important because it gives people the ability to see, and taste, what the world has to offer and how places differ from one another. It gives us information about locations and wines that we might otherwise not have access to. In a sense, it places every vineyard in our backyard. Even if we cannot buy directly online where we live, the knowledge that we attain via the Internet can be taken directly to our favorite wine retailer. As an example, let's say that our local wine retailer does not normally carry any wines from Austria. On the Internet we can find websites from the Wachau, Kamptal, and Kremstal wine regions near the villages of Krems and Langenlois in Austria (very pretty countryside northwest of Vienna). If we really want to try their regional specialty, Grüner Veltliner, we can either buy it online or go to our favorite wine shop and ask them to order the wine for us. The Internet allows us to shop the world.

Although the Internet has had a great impact on the wine industry, it has not put the local wine retailer out of business. Even if we can buy wine online, the local retailer provides an immediacy of purchase that we cannot get online. Our local wine retailers also provide other goods and services that are of value to us, such as wine tastings, face-to-face contact, and advice that goes beyond the anonymity of the Internet. This assumes, of course, that your local retailer provides such services. If not, and if you have enough lead time, then travel the world of wine via the computer and learn what it has to offer.

AUSTRALIA

If any place has benefited from the changing retail geography of wine it is Australia. Twenty years ago you might have been hard-pressed to find a bottle of Australian wine at your local wine shop. That is definitely not the case today. If your wine shop is anything like mine, it has dozens and dozens of different Australian wines. Most are from large wineries, but wines from smaller wineries are beginning to sneak in.

There are some very good reasons for the growing presence of Australian wine. First, Australia has a climate for almost every kind of grape. Also, many of the Australian winemakers are descendents of winemakers who emigrated to Australia from wine regions in Europe, and winemaking is in their blood. For those who are not of winemaking families, Australia has an educational system that has turned out incredibly knowledgeable and ambitious vintners and winemakers who have achieved great success with their wines. Australian winemakers have also been quick to adopt the latest technologies. These factors, along with effective marketing and pricing, have enabled Australian vintners to make their wines household names. Even though Australia is literally a world away from consumers in North America and Europe, their wines are everywhere.

The retailing of Australian wine offers a good example of a product that is in the growth stage of its life cycle. When we talk about the geographic diffusion of a product we often use the life cycle as a basis for the discussion. In the product life cycle, a product is introduced to the market. This introduction starts rather slowly, with limited market penetration, and many products never get past this stage. Products that have an appeal thanks to their quality, the application of new technologies, pricing, or that are simply well-marketed novelties can sometimes take off. Their sales rapidly increase and they begin to appear in markets all over the world. This is where Australian wines are in the product life cycle. They are good, well priced, apply the latest technologies, and are well marketed. So they are in a period of high growth.

Where Australia goes in the product life cycle has yet to be determined. Over time even the best products can saturate the market and lose their novelty; consumers may move on, and want to try the next "new thing." The possibility exists that the growing presence of Australian wines will, indeed, eventually saturate the market. On the other hand, Australian wines could continue to improve through the proliferation of new wines and aggressive marketing. This does not typically occur with food products, but there is always a first time. Maybe Australian wines will be it.

Australia is a very big, very diverse place. In the far north of the country are tropical rain-forest environments. To the south, on the island of Tasmania, the climate is quite cool. In between, there is one of the earth's largest deserts. And although the population of Australia is smaller than some cities, it is still a continent that is almost as large as Europe.

As such, Australia has a tremendous range of growing environments that can accommodate almost any wine varietal. The challenge has been to match the varietals with the right places so that good wine can be produced, and profit made. This matching process involves understanding how the climate of southern Australia is influenced by the westerly winds and cold ocean currents. Most of Australia is desert. Although it may be suitable for some of the world's largest ranching operations, the Outback has little to offer vintners. The focus of viticulture is the thin strip of land nestled south of the desert along the coastline. Just south of Perth, in southwestern Australia, the winds coming off of the cold ocean water create an environment that is well suited to cabernet sauvignon and Shiraz. Farther east, desert conditions predominate and vineyards are absent until we reach Adelaide. From Adelaide northeast into the interior, the region supports cooler-weather grapes such as chardonnay and pinot noir. Off the southern coast, the cold ocean currents and westerly winds make the island of Tasmania the coldest part of Australia. These conditions make Tasmania an ideal match for cool-weather grapes like those common to Alsace and the Rhine River regions in Europe.

Thanks to ocean currents and their impact on Australia's climate, a place can be found for almost any grape. Given the limited population and wide-open spaces, there is the potential for viticulture on a grand scale. They may not have the romance of a Bordeaux château (refinery-like complexes seldom do), but the huge wineries have real economic advantages. They distribute the costs of their operation over an enormous number of bottles of wine, which keeps the cost per bottle relatively low even though the quality of the wine is high. The savings on production covers the increased cost of getting their wines to distant markets. Good quality and competitive prices are what make Australian wines very marketable, which is why it would be a challenge to find a wine store today that did not offer a nice array of Australian wines.

Chapter 13

COMMUNISM, GEOGRAPHY, AND WINE

When I talk about the impacts of communism on commodities like wine, I am often asked, "Isn't communism dead?" The truth is that communism is not dead. It is just that the case studies are getting to be rather scarce. Even if there were no communist governments, no communist parties, no communist politicians, and no communist intellectuals left anywhere, communism would still exist. Communism leaves an imprint on the landscape just like any other economic system. So even if communism was dead, there would still be places where we would see its remains. This is especially true in the wine-producing regions of eastern Europe.

Communism changes one of the fundamental assumptions that we use in economic geography and in reading the cultural landscape—that decisions are made based on individuals and their desire to make a profit. This does not apply in communism. Communism is about equity and the human condition. It is about improving the lives of all individuals by improving health, education, employment, housing, and so on, regardless of their ability to pay. This is by no means a bad idea. The problem with communism has always been figuring out how to make it work. For viticulture and other forms of agriculture in communist countries, the government is in charge. It maintains tight planning of inputs, outputs, inventories, and targets development considered important to the overall economy. These systems are often closed to market economies. Domestic markets are prioritized first, trade with other communist economies second, and trade outside the communist realm is considered only when necessary. This has had the effect of isolating wine producers within communist countries from consumers in market economies.

Within communist economies the central government establishes production priorities for both the short and long term. From these plans it determines yearly production targets, develops plans, and sets control figures (quotas) for output. It then sends those figures out to subordinate agencies that control the various branches of the economy and which determine the input requirements necessary to meet the quotas. These requirements are then sent back up the hierarchy, numbers are crunched, and the commodity exchanges needed to meet the targets set by the government are determined. Everyone works to meet the targets come hell or high water. Then the whole thing starts over again. With regard to winemaking, the government tells vintners what to produce, and they, in turn, tell the government what they need to produce it. The government gets them what they need, and everybody is (supposedly) happy.

The first step of this process occurs when the central government establishes the priorities of the economy. It is not like in a market system where people decide what to produce based on profit potential. In practical application the result has been an emphasis on heavy industry, defense, and self-sufficiency. This has come at the cost of consumer goods. And as a consumer good, wine production has always been considered a low-level priority. Consequently, it has often been slighted in favor of other forms of production.

We can criticize communism for the creation of huge government bureaucracies. A more telling problem has been that it has created what free-market economists see as very dysfunctional behavior. As applied, branch agencies in communist economies are responsible for production, distribution, personnel, and research and development, as well as worker housing, plan fulfillment, and resource allocation. More important, they are in charge of making sure that their constituent industries meet their quotas. This responsibility is where the problems start.

Let us say that we are responsible for the production of a certain number of a particular item. We are successful in our work if we meet our quota, and we fail if we do not. If we want to avoid failure, are there any preventative measures that we can take? One way is to make sure that the quota is attainable year in and year out. If we go crazy one year and double our production, it is a pretty good bet that our quota will go up. If that situation continues we may eventually reach a point where we cannot meet our quota. The lesson here is to make our quota, but do not exceed it. We may also want to hoard materials and labor so that we do not have supply problems that could cause us to miss our quota. We may also want to reconsider those activities that cut back on overall production. Upgrading our facility could cost us production time. Producing varieties of sizes and styles to meet the needs of every consumer will also cut our overall production as we retool our facility. As the year comes to a close we may need to storm (or cram) in order to meet our quota, whether or not huge amounts of the item we have produced are needed at that time of year. This strategy allowed us to reach our quota but it may not do much for the overall productivity of the economy.

In communist societies, wine producers are pretty low on the pecking order because they produce consumer goods that are associated with wealth. For a time during the Gorbachev era, wine and all other alcohols were considered a societal evil. The support of winemakers was therefore one of the lowest economic priorities of the government; they received limited resources, and suffered from labor shortages. In addition, the brightest minds of the country migrated to better jobs in the high-priority sectors of the economy.

Against this backdrop of deprivation winemakers faced the challenge of producing a set volume of wine, their quota. Great wines produced in small amounts did no good whatsoever. Old vineyards taken out of production for replanting reduced production and the chances of meeting quota. New vineyards brought into production used high-yield rather than high-quality grapes. High-quality grapes already planted were mixed with lesser-quality grapes to even out—not necessarily improve—quality. Aging wine over long time periods was bad for the quota. The end result was a system where the taste of the wine was secondary. Repeating this over a long period of communist rule impoverished the wine industry. Even in eastern European countries with flourishing wine industries before communism (Hungary,

Bulgaria, Romania, and Czechoslovakia), the lack of investment and the struggle to make quotas brought the industry to its knees.

The problem with communism has not been restricted to viticulture. The truth is that communism has had a tough time dealing with agriculture in general. As with other sectors of the economy, agriculture is controlled by central authorities. The state exercises decision-making power over agricultural land use, what is planted, where it is planted, procurement price, product marketing, and product distribution. While in theory this should work, reality never quite caught up to the theory. This was especially true in the Soviet Union. Prior to communism agricultural decisions had been made at the local level by the very same wealthy landowners who fought against the communists in the revolution. Putting this power in the hands of a terribly poor peasantry did not do much good. They did not have the infrastructure needed to produce much more than they were already producing. The solution was to collectivize agriculture. This was meant to alleviate the problem by putting agriculture under government control and consolidating peasant holdings into collective farms. These could then be treated like individual factories for the purpose of assigning quotas.

The problem was that there was almost no vested interest in the product. In a market economy, wages and profit provide an incentive for maximizing output. The rule is the harder you work the more you get. In a communist economy the same wage was paid whether you were the world's best farmer or the worst. The unfortunate result is that everyone ends up working down to the lowest level. Farms in market economies produce so much food that government has to step in to buy up the excess or to pay farmers not to farm, while farmers in a communist system, given the same environmental constraints, may not produce enough to feed their people.

It is important to emphasize that the problem was not that the people could not produce food. Actually, it is quite the contrary. When given the opportunity to produce their own food on private plots of land, they produced amazing quantities, enough for themselves and sufficient surpluses for a flourishing informal market. Problems arose when people left their farming jobs to work on their private plots, a situation that underscored the fact that the farmers were not deficient, they just needed the right incentives.

Since the fall of the Iron Curtain, farmers have been set loose in a very competitive market. Those who previously had worked in a low-productivity environment, where they could produce lesser-quality products, struggled because poorly produced products do not sell in the free market. The pace of transition from a communist to a free-market economy has varied from place to place and from economic sector to economic sector, but the challenges remain the same. There have been complicated questions over who actually owns the farms. There have also been issues of unemployment when societies make the transition from a high-labor system to one that is highly mechanized. Even where these problems have been dealt with there is the problem of start-up funding. Where does the money come from to build an agricultural enterprise capable of competing in the free market?

For better or worse, the transition to a free-market economy has forced former communist countries into a reliance on resource exports. Due to the inefficiencies of the quota system, the heavy industries that were at the heart of the communist economies have faltered in the face of free-market competition. Resource trade has not faced the same difficulties. This is because oil is oil. Coal is coal. Timber is timber. We do not see the same kinds of product variations that we do in consumer electronics or cars. This market change has accompanied a change in the geographic pattern of trade. Prior to the fall of communism, most trade was in heavy industrial products. It was internal or within the communist world. Trade was part of foreign relations and was competitive, but only within the communist world. It was kept separate from the free-market economies. In the postcommunist era that pattern has changed. The trading partners are now with the economic powers of the free market. In those trading relationships the former communist countries are often dealing from a position of weakness.

The reliance on resource exports puts the former communist countries in an unenviable position, placing them into competition with the nations of the third world. Their only worthwhile export is their natural resource endowment. The exported resources are used in manufacturing elsewhere. It is in that manufacturing where most of the profit is found. This gives the wealthy capitalist economies the upper hand. They can buy resources from whatever providers sell the cheapest. Everyone who exports the resource is in competition. It makes the pricing of commodities extremely variable and allows the wealthy capitalist countries to dictate prices. As the natural resource is simply an input in the production of manufactured goods, the resource exporters become dependent on the resource importers. The proceeds from resource sales are used to buy expensive manufactured goods from the very same wealthy capitalist countries that bought the resources. The result can be a pattern of spiraling debt that is only exacerbated by the actions of the lending industry.

This brings us back to wine as an object of trade. On the one hand, wine is very much like a resource. A quality product can compete in the free market. Given low labor costs in the former communist economies, they may even be able to undersell their competition on the free market. As such, wine production is a potentially profitable activity for countries trying to gain their economic footing in a free market. Of course, none of that can happen unless product quality reaches a competitive level.

EASTERN EUROPE

When we talk about wines and go to wine tastings, the wines of Hungary, Bulgaria, Romania, and Moldova usually do not come up in our conversations. The fact that their wines are not well known outside eastern Europe is not because these countries are new to winemaking. Each has a proud history of wine production that extends back many hundreds of years. Their wines graced the cellars of the Romanoffs and the Hapsburgs. It is just that fifty years of communism have had a severe impact on their wines.

Climatically there is a significant range of conditions for winemaking in eastern Europe. Northern Romania and Moldova are on the northern fringe of winemaking. As we move south, conditions warm up markedly. This is a product of latitude as well as of topography. The Carpathian Mountains and Transylvanian Alps serve as a divide between the cold winter climates to the north and the more moderate climates to the south. The Black Sea helps also to moderate climatic conditions in these countries. As we move farther south into Bulgaria we are approaching the kinds of Mediterranean climates under which *Vitis vinifera* can flourish.

While eastern European wine producers make an interesting if depressing study of the effects communism had on wine, much more interesting is what is going on with them today. There is now a history of successful wine production in the region. Fans of sweet wines might already be familiar with Tokay grapes of southeastern Hungary and the wines that they produce. Many other varietals have traditionally been part of winemaking in the region. Unfortunately they are virtually unknown to consumers outside the region. More than that, there is a climate that will support most of the popular wine grape varietals.

With the expansion of the European Union into eastern Europe, and the opportunities provided by climates in this region, the rebirth of the local wine industry is in progress. Except for Moldova, all of the aforementioned countries (Hungary, Bulgaria, and Romania) have achieved EU membership, though they will not adopt the euro until their economies and currencies are stabilized. For now, there is the benefit of EU membership which provides a secure investing environment, and favorable exchange rates with the present national currencies. The climate and history of wine production support the potential for investment. For vintners and enologists trained elsewhere in the EU, these new member states provide opportunities for employment that might not be available in their home countries.

The fall of communism in eastern Europe exposed the wine producers of the region to direct competition in the world market. The result for many other industries was complete collapse. For wine it has created a potentially lucrative investment environment. As wine consumers these circumstances may not affect us now, but it might in the future as we begin to see eastern European wines appearing in our favorite wine stores.

GEOGRAPHY AND WINE'S COMPETITORS: BEER, CIDER, AND DISTILLED SPIRITS

The nice thing about geography is that you can turn almost any interest into the subject of study. This is true for the Bible, quilting, duckpin bowling, zydeco, and even wine.

The geography of wine is a broad enough subject on its own. Expanding the subject to include all the different alcohols produced for human consumption would be an undertaking of encyclopedic proportions. In some sense it is also unnecessary, since the importance of environment and culture in the production of wine is mirrored in the production of other alcohols. We need only discuss a few exemplars of wine's competitors in order to understand the basic geography they all share.

The geography of wine's competitors has a great deal to do with environment. Over time a place becomes home to a certain kind of alcohol production, by dint of climate, soil, agriculture, or any of the other considerations that we have discussed. We associate vodka with Russia, tequila with Mexico, and rum with Jamaica. Alcohol is one of the physical manifestations, or "traits" of the culture. We not only recognize the link between place, people, and culture, but we perpetuate them. By selecting the culturally appropriate drink to accompany a specific ethnic cuisine, we are keeping those cultural associations alive.

Culture is traditionally the realm of anthropology. Geography comes into the picture because cultural traits (things, ideas, and beliefs) and cultural complexes (groups of interlocking traits) have spatial manifestations. Because cultural traits and complexes are also capable of movement, culture is something that can be mapped by geographers. It has patterns that we can study and attempt to understand. A culture, linked to the places where it is found, leaves an imprint on the landscape and, in turn, is imprinted by that landscape.

THE COMPETITION

Wine is a part of many different cultures. However, in terms of people, places, and production, its influence is dwarfed by that of beer. Beer is one of the world's most common alcoholic drinks. As a low-alcohol beverage it is comparable to and in some cases interchangeable with wine, but the geographies of beer and wine are distinctly different. This is due primarily to the use of barley in the production of beer.

Beer is made from barley that has been soaked long enough for the starches in the grain to break down and begin to ferment. It is the link to barley that determines the geography of beer production. In some places beer and wine production overlap. These are areas where both grapes and barley can be grown profitably. The reason that they coexist is that both can be grown in grape-friendly climates.

Von Thunen wrote that when we factor in environment, knowledge, and government regulation, the most profitable crop remaining will be the one that is produced. In this case, why doesn't the most profitable crop win out? The reason is that while grapes and barley can be grown in the same climate, they are not adapted to the same conditions of soil and topography. Grapes do best in well-drained soils and can thrive in places where virtually nothing else will grow. For grapes, what the soil is like far below the surface is key. Barley on the other hand does best in soil that has a good mix of sand, silt, and clay at the surface. Therefore, even in regions that produce grapes and barley, the fields will be physically separate.

One environmental advantage of barley is that it is a grain and not a liquid-rich fruit, and thus is far less susceptible to frost damage than grapes. Barley also has a range of planting options. Winter barley is planted in the late fall or early winter. The seeds are in place and ready to germinate as soon as conditions improve in the spring. Spring barley is planted as soon as conditions permit in the springtime. These planting options give barley a wider potential range of climates. If we have a very short summer, we plant winter barley with an eye toward harvest just before the end of the following summer. This gives us the ability to grow barley profitably in the prairie provinces of Canada, in Scotland, Scandinavia, and parts of central Russia. If our season is longer we plant a conventional spring crop for harvest in the fall. If we have a much longer growing season, we may even be able to get in two barley crops each year (a winter crop harvested in late spring and a spring crop harvested in late fall). As a result, barley can be grown over a much wider area than grapes, and can be used to produce beer over a much wider area as well.

In addition to the range of environments over which it can be produced, barley has a significant advantage over wine in the geography of its production. Grapes have sugars suspended in liquid that can easily begin to ferment whether we want them to or not. As we have seen, this is a significant liability when transporting grapes. It is why the winery is as close to the vineyards as possible. Barley, on the other hand, will not start to ferment on its own without the introduction of water. As long as it is kept dry, barley can be transported long distances prior to its use in beer production. This means that we can produce beer in any location where we can ship barley. Even if the areas that produce grapes and barley are the same, the locations where wine and beer are produced could be very different.

Like wine, beer has its own geography of tastes and styles. A beer can be a stout, ale, bitter, or be made in any of a number of other styles. Even if two beers are of the same style the tastes can be very different. The styles and tastes of beer can differ from one location to another. Even how the beer is served may have its own geography. Like wines and spirits, beers, beer styles, and flavors become associated with places. They also become linked to the foods and, more broadly, the cultures of those places. This makes beer an interesting subject for geographers.

Beer is not the only competitor for wine. Wines produced from other fruits are competitors of wine from grapes. Purists may not recognize these nongrape competitors as being true wines, but depending on issues of climate and geology, these alternatives may be the only means of producing alcohols locally.

If we take fruit juice and store it for a time at room temperature it will eventually begin to ferment. It is not all that difficult to do. Sometimes the difficult part is actually preventing the fermentation. This is the basis for using fruits other than grapes in the winemaking process. In Hawaii there are people who produce pineapple wine. In New England there are wineries that produce cranberry wine. In some cases the use of fruits other than grapes in the production of wine is historically or climatically based. In others, wine production from other fruits is based on the simple fact it can be done.

Long before anyone considered making wine from cranberries, cider was the dominant fruit alcohol drink here in New England. When we use the term "cider" today, we are usually referring to a nonalcoholic apple cider. In other parts of the world, and in the early history of North America, the term "cider" was used for a fermentation of apple juice. Today we typically reserve the term "hard cider" for the alcoholic drink. Before beer became so popular, cider consumption was widespread. In fact, before the advent of refrigeration and pasteurization it would have been almost impossible to store apple juice in a nonalcoholic form. The alcoholic version would have been quite common in areas where there were significant apple producers. Cider may not be as popular or common today but we can still find it being produced in New England, southern England, and northern France.

Because the apple varieties used to produce cider are different from those used for eating or baking, the production of cider requires a choice of apple at the time of tree planting. Cider production is also a long-term process. It can take many years before apple trees are capable of producing useful crops. Damage to the trees can set back harvests for years. This puts cider producers at a distinct disadvantage as compared to beer and even wine producers. Vintners can have vines in production within a few years. Barley is a single-season product. Recalling von Thunen, we can see that these concerns become important when deciding whether to produce cider. They can affect the profitability of the product and its ability to compete with wine, beer, and other alcohols.

Cider, like beer and wine, has a variety of different tastes and styles. In some places cider is a low-alcohol beverage. In others it is produced with an alcohol content well in excess of wine and beer. It can be produced clear and sparkling or cloudy in appearance. From region to region there also will be differences in how the cider is served. All of these factors give cider a geography that is distinct from that of beer or wine.

Of wine's competitors, the most recent are distilled spirits. Distilled spirits begin life in much the same way as other alcoholic beverages: with fermentation. What makes them different is that after the initial fermentation the liquids are distilled into their final form. The distillation process varies little from place to place, but what is being distilled can vary a great deal, which is why the geography of different distilled spirits can vary even though the distillation process is the same.

The process of distillation is based on an important bit of chemistry. Water, depending on the altitude, boils at 212 degrees Fahrenheit. Alcohol, on the other hand, boils at 175 degrees. What this means is that if we take wine, or beer, or cider and heat them to just over 175 degrees, the alcohol will boil off. The alcohol does not disappear; it just changes states. It evaporates.

In distillation we take advantage of the difference in boiling points to produce a high-alcohol product. Theoretically this is not a complex task, though making it work does have a few tricky parts. First, we need to heat the alcohol-bearing liquid above 175 degrees so that the alcohol will evaporate. At the same time we need to keep the temperature below 212 degrees so that the water does not evaporate. If the temperature is too hot, everything boils off and we have distilled nothing. If we have a steady heat source and accurate temperature measurement, then we can control heating to create an alcohol vapor. That brings us to the second tricky part. We have to be able to trap the alcohol vapor without it escaping into the atmosphere. If we can capture that vapor and cool it, then the alcohol will condense back into a liquid. The condensate will have a much higher alcohol content than was present in the original liquid. Our distillation is complete.

The technological hurdles involved in making distilled spirits (steady heating, accurate temperature control, and the ability to trap escaping alcohol vapors) are significant. Prior to the Industrial Revolution overcoming them was extremely difficult. Even if distillation could be accomplished, without accurate controls it was nearly impossible to standardize the product of that distillation. With industrialization, technologies became available that solved these problems, which allowed for large-scale distillation. Accordingly, we associate the proliferation of distilled spirits with industrialization. As we shall see in the next chapter, we also associate it with a growing awareness of alcoholism and the birth of temperance movements.

Even though the processes and principles of distillation are common across places and cultures, there is still a strong geography to it. That is because what is being distilled, and the geography of the source material, will connect the distillation process to specific places. The distilled alcohols will vary in taste, smell, and appearance based on their source materials. Thus, a distillate from a wine source (cognac) will have a different geography and flavor from a sugar cane distillate (rum), a barley mash distillate (whisky), a wheat distillate (vodka), or a blue agave distillate (tequila). Even if the same original source material is used, there may be additives to the process that are common to a place. In that way cognac will be different than ouzo even though both are wine distillates.

SCOTLAND

If anything is associated with Scotland besides cool wet weather, it is whisky. It is a product that is part of their culture, a reflection of the people and the environment of Scotland. There are those who would lump together whisky, rye, scotch, bourbon, and Irish whisky. But to others who love and revere whisky, the view that whisky is interchangeable with anything else would be akin to telling a wine lover that all red wines are the same.

Before we get into the whiskies of Scotland, there is some important geography tied into the name of the product. If it is from Scotland or Ireland it is *whisky*. If it is produced anywhere else it is a *whiskey*, even if it is produced in a Scottish or Irish style. In North America we shorten "Scottish Whisky" into Scotch, assuming that the whisky was produced, aged, and bottled in Scotland. To avoid any social blunders it is also important to remember that the drink is Scotch, the people are Scottish.

Whisky is distilled from barley. This makes it different from bourbon and rye. Bourbon is a corn distillation. Rye is produced from a distillation of at least 50 percent rye grain. The process of distillation and the machinery of that distillation might be interchangeable. The use of barley, corn, or rye makes them distinct. The end result may have a similar appearance, but the use of different starches as a base for the process will result in very different tastes and will produce very different geographies. This is because corn-producing regions are different from those that produce barley and/or rye.

It is not simply the naming or the starch that distinguishes these products. Some distinctions are based on the fuel used in the distillation process and the exposure of the barley malts to the fuel smoke. In Scotland and Ireland peat is a common fuel for the distillation process. Peat is an accumulation of partially decomposed organic matter that we find in cool semiwetland environments. When dried and cut into bricks, peat becomes a fuel source. Given the geographic limitation of peat bogs, we find peat as a fuel source for whisky but not for bourbon. That is because corn production and peat bogs are found in distinctly different climates. In the drying of the barley malt the use of peat becomes an important element in distinguishing between Scottish and Irish whiskies. In Scotland the malt is exposed to the peat smoke. In Ireland it is not. This exposure influences the taste of the product and is what distinguishes the two whiskies. Even if the whisky is produced in the same manner, differences in the peat may be discernable in the taste of the final product.

Even if we use the same grains, the same fuel source, and the same distillation process, the resulting whisky may still be distinct from all others. Minute differences in the chemical composition of the water used in the distillation process are reflected in the taste of the resulting whisky. As such, water is to whisky like soil is to wine. Even minor variations make a difference. Distilleries in close proximity to one another can produce distinctly different products based on the qualities of their water.

Whisky is aged, sometimes over long time periods. Aging changes the taste and appearance of the whisky such that small variations in the initial product can be magnified with time. As with wine, whisky can pick up tastes from the barrels it is aged in. Aging will result in the loss of some whisky through evaporation from the porous barrels. The porosity of the barrels is such that prolonged aging may allow the outside air to influence the look and taste of the final product. What the whiskies lose in volume they gain in taste and appearance through the aging process.

The geography of Scottish whisky is thus a combination of the geographies of barley, peat, water, and even air, all of which affects the product and links the whisky to the place where it is produced. Each of Scotland's whisky regions is distinct; it is akin to *terroir* and wine. If you have seen one you have definitely not seen them all. As such, it makes for good tourism. What also makes for good tourism is that whiskies are produced all over Scotland. From the Orkney Islands in the north to the southernmost lowland distilleries, you are never far from a distillery in Scotland.

The interesting thing about distilleries in Scotland is that they can be found in some of the most inaccessible places. Yes, there are quite a few lowland distilleries near Glasgow and Edinburgh, and dozens of them in the valley of the Spey River (the Speyside distilleries) east of Inverness. Then again, there are also distilleries scattered about in every nook and cranny of the

Highlands. All share the common geography of proximity to sources of barley, peat, and the availability of fresh water.

Perhaps the most inaccessible of the whisky regions of Scotland, and for my money the most interesting, are the island distilleries off the west coast. There are active distilleries on the islands of Mull, Skye, Jura, and Arran. Outnumbering them all are the distilleries on the Isle of Islay. Islay and the other islands are barren and stark but yet still have a beauty to them. They do not have highway access and are off the beaten track, accessible only by small ferries on rather limited schedules. This means that they are not heavily traveled by tourists, making them ideal for an out-of-the-way vacation of nature walks, whale and wildlife watching, biking, and distillery visits. The fact that many of the islands also have Iron Age and Stone Age archeological remains as well as significant early Christian sites makes them that much more interesting. Their isolation and the connections between the people and their surroundings, including those who work in the distilleries, give the communities and their distilleries a "one with the earth" kind of charm. While the distilleries may be industrial, their feel is anything but.

Understanding wine allows us to look at its competitors in a whole new light. We do not need to start from scratch if we want to examine the geographies of beer, cider, or distilled spirits. All we need to grasp how each of these alcohols is different from wine is to use our knowledge of wine as a bridge to understanding its competitors. We may never have the same appreciation for distilled spirits that we do for wine, but we can still appreciate their geographies.

Chapter 15

WINE, CULTURE, AND THE
GEOGRAPHY OF TEMPERANCE

In some societies wine is part of family life and it would be unusual not to see it at the dinner table. In other societies wine is strictly for adults or for religious practice and is viewed as separate from family life. The way that cultures vary in their treatment of food products in general and wine in particular makes for some fascinating geography. We could literally spend a lifetime studying when, where, how, and why people drink wine.

One of the more interesting areas of research into the links between wine and culture deals with the influence of religion. In some religions wine and other alcohols are prohibited. In others, wine is an integral part of the practice. The link between the history of wine, religious practice, and religious institutions is especially strong in the Catholic Church, which is widely credited with preserving and advancing the wine industry after the fall of the Roman Empire. This is not because the end of the empire accompanied a decline in alcohol consumption. Rather, the end of the empire, with the coming of conflict and political instability, meant a disruption of the economic system and commercial linkages that had moved wine around the Roman world. Centuries later, as man emerged from the Dark Ages, exploration, missionary work, and colonization took sacramental wine and grapes to the far corners of the globe. But throughout history wine has been much more than a luxury item or an element for religious ceremony. It has been a beverage, for regular consumption, much as we consume water today. In some places and times it was a much safer drink than water. So compared to the amount of wine consumed in a community on an average day, the sacramental use of wine would have been exceedingly limited. Why then is there a historical link between the Church and wine?

The link between the Church and wine is one of economics. Throughout European history, the Church has traditionally been a major landholder. In life and in death people donated land to the Church. They also paid the Church for services in land. The end result was that the Church owned a heck of a lot of property. This raised the question that we asked in our discussion of von Thunen and the geography of agriculture. What use of the land would produce the best return? It could be used to generate regular income or it could be sold for a one-time infusion of cash. The cash would be good if there was a specific need for it. Economically the better long-term decision was and is income generation. For the Church, wine production was the best answer.

In addition to the economic issues of holding and using land, we could also look at the Church as a major player in the science of wine. Human creativity and inventiveness have always benefited from an environment where people have the time and opportunity to think. By attracting the best and brightest minds of their day and by affording them the opportunity they needed to generate ideas, the Church played a significant role in the developing sciences of viticulture and winemaking. It was not because the Church purposefully set out to pioneer the production of new grape varietals, to test planting techniques, or to create a better wine bottle. Rather, it was the unintentional effect of allowing great minds to pursue their interests and innovations. The possibility that these innovations might be of financial benefit to the Church would have given added impetus to the work of these learned individuals.

RELIGION, FOOD TABOOS, AND CULTURAL GEOGRAPHY

It is interesting that while one religion embraces wine as an element of religious ceremony, another religion can take a very different approach. Some religions may completely prohibit certain food and drink items or have periodic restrictions linked to a time of year or a holiday. As part of the geography of culture, food and drink preferences that are expressed in religion alter some of our basic geographic assumptions. They change the geography of agriculture and force us to consider how culture influences our choice of what to grow and what to produce. In terms of religion and its impact on the geography of wine, we can see how the Church fostered the development and spread of the wine industry. By comparison we can also look at the effect that Islam has had on that very same industry. Rather than linking wine to religious practice, in Islam alcohol consumption is forbidden. As such, discussing Islam and wine is very appropriate for a chapter on the geography of temperance.

Restrictions against alcohol consumption in Islam are very interesting for those of us who are students of the geography of wine. The Islamic nations of the Middle East are in climatic regions that would be very good for wine production. Some of the same places that were centers for winemaking a few thousand years ago are today located within countries with no meaningful wine production. That is not to say that these countries do not produce grapes. Grapes and grape juice are perfectly acceptable. They are just not used to produce wine. What this does is to add another element to von Thunen's model of agriculture: that the highest-value use for a crop we have the knowledge and/or equipment to grow may not be socially acceptable to our culture.

The influence of Islam on wine is also interesting for its impact on trade and on areas that were once part of the Islamic world. In Spain and Portugal, a flourishing wine industry dating back to the time of the ancient Greeks disappeared with the Moorish conquest of the Iberian peninsula in the seventh and eighth centuries. The same could be said for eastern Europe prior to its conquest by the Ottoman Turks. The conquest of Granada in 1492 ended the Moorish occupation of Spain. In eastern Europe, Ottoman control over wine-producing regions persisted through the nineteenth and early twentieth centuries. The disruption of the wine industry in these regions occurred at the same time that the urban wine markets of western and northern Europe were just coming into their own.

In spite of religious taboos against wine consumption, the Middle East is not devoid of wine production. In some areas winemaking persists thanks to demand and the economic expectations of profit. In other areas wine production is indicative of wider social and cultural differences in the region. Areas of wine production may indicate the presence of non-Islamic peoples, and wine is thus part of the religious and cultural diversity of the region.

Food and drink taboos make for some interesting geography, and they are made even more interesting by the fact that they can change over time. This is very true of wine and the temperance movement. As previously discussed, in early societies alcoholic beverages like wine were an alternative to water, as it was safe from diseases such as cholera that were commonly associated with contaminated water supplies. This began to change with industrialization and the mass production of distilled spirits. The availability and affordability of high-alcohol products led to a proliferation of alcohol problems in the population, which, in turn, led to a greater understanding of alcoholism as a disease and a social ill. Coupled with massive urban population growth and grinding poverty, the growing awareness of alcoholism led to the growth of the temperance movement.

The temperance movement of the late nineteenth and early twentieth centuries was not identical in all places. Maybe some countries became industrialized so quickly that the availability of distilled spirits and the problems they caused were magnified. Maybe other countries never shifted very far from the idea of wine and beer as acceptable beverages for regular consumption. Or maybe some countries' economies relied on wine and beer production. Whatever the cause, the geographic impact of the temperance movement was quite varied.

Even in societies that embraced temperance, wine was distinguished from other forms of alcohol. Its medicinal and sacramental uses placed it on a higher level than other forms of alcohol. It also had a higher class of users, or at least that was its reputation. Along with beer, wine was viewed as a food product. So wine and beer were often ignored by temperance advocates in favor of cutting the consumption of higher-alcohol products.

In the United States the temperance movement took a turn that was very different from the rest of the world, encouraging the prohibition of high-alcohol drinks as well as wine and beer. The culmination of that effort was the ratification of the Volstead Act (the Eighteenth Amendment) that in 1919 led to Prohibition.

Even before the imposition of the Volstead Act most states were already dry. What the Volstead Act did was make the rest of the country dry. In spite of efforts to exclude wine, it too was restricted by Prohibition. Though there were loopholes for medicinal and sacramental wine production, the level of wine production for such uses or for the sale of table grapes was nowhere near what was necessary to sustain the wine industry. The repeal of Prohibition in 1933 came too late to save most wine producers. Nor did it legalize the sale of alcohol. All it did was to place the matter back in the hands of state governments. This created an interesting geography of wet and dry states that persisted until 1966 (when the last dry state—Mississippi—went wet). State decisions to permit alcohol sales did not mean that all of their constituent communities approved. Even today there remain many counties that are dry.

Nowadays, relatively few people remember the repeal of the Volstead Act (the Twenty-first Amendment) in 1933, not to mention its imposition in 1919. Even so, the effects of Prohibition are still geographically relevant today. Although Prohibition ended, the regulation of alcohol sales remains a state and local concern. As such, the geography of wine and especially the geography of wine retailing may vary considerably based on the local regulatory environment. Dry counties are often ringed with liquor stores located barely a few feet over the county line. Differences in state "sin taxes" on alcohol and tobacco result in an interesting assortment of Interstate highway rest stops along state borders. The signs might as well read "welcome to [*insert state name here*]. Liquor and alcohol sales 1 mile ahead." There are even states where liquor is sold through state vendors; arguably, this may provide greater control over liquor sales. But from personal experience I have never found direct state intervention in alcohol sales to be good for service or selection.

AMERICA EAST OF THE ROCKIES

If there was any wine industry winner that came out of the temperance movement and Prohibition, it was definitely California. Although the industry was virtually wiped out elsewhere, California managed to survive in an operational form. In most of the rest of the country, the wine industry has been clawing its way back so that it now exceeds pre-Prohibition levels. Modern advances in winemaking have in some areas created opportunities for entrepreneurs to build vineyards and wineries in areas that had no wine production before Prohibition. Moreover, some very recent changes in federal legislation have allowed for a flowering of the wine industry around the United States.

Although it may not be the most important piece of legislation for the wine industry, the Farm Winery Act of 1976 should hold a special place in your heart. It paved the way for direct sales of wine from small wineries to visitors and consumers around the country, and decreased the fees and red tape involved in winery development. The rights guaranteed in the act have subsequently been strengthened by revisions that now protect the sale of wines from such producers via the Internet. The effect of this regulation is to permit small wineries to bypass wine merchants and to sell direct to the public. It has also provided an incentive for winery tourism. Without this regulation, visitors to a winery might be able to buy mementos of their visit but no wine. Now wineries have an incentive to bring in visitors. A short tour of the vineyard and winery can be followed by a tasting of the products and direct sales to the visitors. Prior to the Farm Winery Act this activity would have triggered a visit from the local representatives of the federal Bureau of Alcohol, Tobacco, and Firearms.

The relaxation of government restrictions on the wine industry has fueled a rapid growth in the number of U.S. wineries. This growth has been fostered not only by the Farm Winery Act, but by the ability of wineries to import grapes. With imported grapes a winery can begin production while newly planted vineyards mature. This reduces the waiting time necessary to begin seeing profits from investment in planting and material purchases and eases some of the economic burden involved in establishing new wineries.

The number of wineries now in operation in the United States, as well as the number of states that now produce wine, has increased dramatically. There are probably more states that produce wine today than there are states that do not. A quick visit to the Internet will yield information on wineries in Iowa, Michigan, Pennsylvania, Virginia, North Carolina, Rhode Island, Maine, New Hampshire, Massachusetts, Texas, Ohio, Arizona, Connecticut, and many others. In big wine-producing states such as New York, we can see the proliferation of wine along the southern shore of the Great Lakes and into the Hudson Valley. There has also been a flood of new vineyards on Long Island. Given the rapid growth of the industry, U.S. wine now exceeds pre-Prohibition levels of wine production. It has also spread to areas that were not wine producers prior to Prohibition.

The wide variety of places in the United States that produce wine is such that it is tough to make many generalizations. The range of climates provides opportunities for producing almost any kind of wine grape. The choice depends on finding the best grape for the climate. American universities and state extension services have become very active players in this process of matching places and grapes. As new vineyards and wineries come into operation it will take a while for their products to enter the mainstream. Until then, new wineries develop from a base of local markets (wine stores and restaurants) as well as from direct sales to visitors. So it may be difficult to find some of the newest wines in our local wine shops.

The proliferation of wine in the United States is still in its infancy and is strongly regional, with much local character in the people, products, and facilities involved. Wine consumers in other parts of the country may simply not be familiar with all of them. It is important for wine regions to have an identity, at least from a marketing perspective. We know what to expect when we buy wine from well-known wine regions, but most consumers' knowledge of wines from Ohio, Arizona, or Connecticut begins and ends with the fact that they are not from California. This may be a hard thing to overcome in marketing their wines, but we can put a positive spin on it. If we are interested in wines and curious about the places that produce them, the differences in regional production may be enough to draw our attention. It gives us an incentive to experience them all. Who knows? In doing so we may stumble upon the next great place for wine.

Chapter 16

REGIONAL IDENTITY, WINE, AND MULTINATIONALS

Imagine being at a party where there is an open bar complete with numerous spirits and liqueurs. There are a few dozen different wines representing vineyards in Italy, California, Australia, and New Zealand. There are also more beer choices than we can keep track of. As we face the daunting task of choosing what to drink, it may never occur to us that all of these wines, beers, and spirits may come from the same company. Regardless of the choice that we make, the bottom line is that our money is going to the same place.

There are a variety of big corporate presences in the alcoholic beverage market. Multinational corporate holdings in the alcoholic beverage industry are growing and companies that traditionally have not been a part of the industry are looking at it with an eye toward diversification and for the acquisition of lucrative labels. It is all part of the new world economic order. For most wine lovers, our idealized image of winemakers does not include major corporations.

Should we care whether our wine is made by a faceless corporate presence with subsidiaries all over the world? This growing multinational presence in the alcoholic beverage industry is a sign of the times. It is rational economic behavior. To those of us who love wine, however, corporate involvement in the alcoholic beverage industry causes some angst. On the one hand, so-called corporate wine may be of high quality, may make use of the best science and technology, and may include well-recognized labels that are aggressively marketed. Corporate involvement may even result in lower pricing through economies of scale. On the other hand, it comes at the expense of our mental picture of the quaint, family-run vineyard. As wine lovers we do not expect our favorite winemakers to be traded on the stock market, to be known for their beer commercials, or to be major corporate sponsors of professional sports. Today they may be.

WINE AND IDENTITY

That we have come to associate certain things with the places that produce them is an interesting phenomenon. Taking that observation one step further, we can see how the quality of a product becomes place associated. A great many places may produce a product, but some may be known for high-quality production while others may be known for poor-quality production. This stereotyping of products and places may or may not be accurate, but it exists nonetheless.

Food products are especially sensitive to place stereotyping. We want foods to come from the places that we associate with them. Even if they are not from that place, the right name or image on the packaging can be enough to persuade us of its quality. Place stereotyping sells. If our favorite beer is made in

Wisconsin, a nice Germanic name and image on the bottle may be enough to convince people that it is worth trying. That may also be why so many wines have French-sounding names and stylized "French" images on the bottles even if they are produced a world away from Bordeaux or Burgundy.

The European Union is an interesting player in the game of place identity and food products. On the one hand, the EU is trying to create a unified Europe. On the other, EU programs stress cultural identity and heritage. While the EU is creating one Europe, it is very active in recognizing the differences that exist within that Europe. For products such as wine and cheese, this means that the desire to create an economically homogenized Europe must contend with regulations that protect the good name of specialized local products.

Protecting the good name of a place is instrumental to the marketing of place-identified food products. Wine and cheese are the most common examples of these. The influences of environment and the creative process involved in their creation have resulted in them being strongly associated (and named after) the places in which they originated. Some names have become so strongly associated with the process for creating the product that the place association has been lost over time. Where such associations still exist, there are regulations to protect them. Champagne is only champagne if it comes from the Champagne region of France. If it does not, it might be labeled as a California champagne (produced by the *méthode champenoise*), a Brut, a sparkling wine, an Asti Spumante, or any number of other localized terms. The reality is that they are all champagnes; they just are not all made *in* Champagne. The idea behind the regulations is that if a product is named after a place then all products that carry that name will contribute to the good or bad name of the place. The argument is that such protection prevents fraud and promotes the integrity of the product. Others argue that protecting the good name of a place is only a convenient excuse for trade protectionism. Of course the folks who run our local wine shops probably do not care much about regulations and trade protectionism. For them and for most wine consumers it is champagne regardless of the legalities involved.

Imitation may be the sincerest form of flattery but sometimes it is just plain fraud. The most obvious form of wine fraud is to use the good name of an existing winemaker to sell a product that they did not make. The fraudulent product is typically of lesser quality. (If it was of better quality why would we need the fraud?) In geographic terms, fraud can also extend to the meaning and identity of a place. For instance, if we want to make the most of our wine sales or to market our wine to a larger population, why not just label it Bordeaux? Bordeaux means quality to consumers, so it will sell. It is a red wine; who will know the difference?

The reality is that it is not just the name of the producer that matters. Wine fraud can also affect a whole region. Fraud can be committed by "stealing" the good name of the region as a means to make money. Just as the name of a producer can convey quality, so can the name of a region. That name can also convey information about the grapes that were used, the combinations of different varietals, and their growing conditions. Saying that we are selling a Bordeaux wine is fraudulent even if we are selling a wine made from grapes that are typical of the Bordeaux region. We may be selling a wine in the Bordeaux style. But we are not selling Bordeaux. Such fraud takes money out of the hands of the real Bordeaux producers and sullies the good name of the region.

The use of Bordeaux as an example in this discussion is not accidental. It is because Bordeaux has historically had a leading role in efforts aimed at preventing wine fraud. Quality wine producers in the region have always had a vested interest in ensuring that their wines were not imitated illegally. This was to protect their reputations as well as their profits. Their efforts led to classification systems for Bordeaux wine, including the châteaux classification system of 1855. Moreover, their work served as the basis for systems of wine classification that have become the standard for the industry.

THE IMPORTANCE AND MEANING OF A LABEL

The information on a wine label conveys a great deal of information. It tells us about the winemaker and the place of origin of the wine. It may even tell us which grape varietals were used. Although those bits of information are fairly straightforward, a good deal of information on the label requires interpretation. This is especially true of wines labeled with place names and that contain references to AOC's, DOC's, or any number of other acronyms.

A wine label bears the name of the maker and should indicate the country of origin. It may also include information on the importer and, depending on where the wine comes from, indicate the dominant grape variety. If the wine is from France it may also include a place name followed by the term AOC. It may only have a place name. Right now I am looking at a bottle of Côtes du Rhône (having wine nearby is very inspirational when writing a wine book). It is a nice red wine and tastes very good. Some people may be able to identify the grape varieties in the wine based on taste alone, but I am definitely not one of those people. So how do I know what I am drinking? In reality the label is communicating that information to me. I just need to understand the language.

The AOC label (*appellation d'origine controllée*) gives us some important information about the wine we are drinking. It tells us that the grapes come from the region identified on the label. If they did not, the wine could not carry that label (it would be fraud). It also tells us something about the grape varietals used. They are the characteristic grape varietals of that place. The only problem is that if we do not know the place, we probably do not know the grape varietals, either. We may have some idea which grapes are used in certain well-known wine regions, but for a lesser-known region or for a region where grape varietals are blended, we may need some help. This is where a good wine atlas will come in handy. I can look up Côtes du Rhône and learn exactly what it is that I am drinking: a wine composed primarily of Syrah, grenache, and Mourvedre grapes. If the wine is made from grapes that are not characteristic of the region, the designation AOC may not be used. The wine would probably be labeled as a table wine from the region in question. At that point your guess is as good as mine as to what is in the bottle. While the example above is from France, we could just as easily have used one from Italy, Spain, or the United States by eliminating AOC and substituting DOC, DO, or AVA, respectively. The acronyms are different, but they all establish a legally recognized link between the wine and a place.

Even for wines labeled by their grape varietals there will still be legally appropriate place designators. They will tell us, for example, that a wine is not just a California chardonnay, but that it is a chardonnay from Napa (the Napa AVA—American Viticultural Area) or Sonoma (Sonoma AVA) or the Central Valley (Central Valley AVA). Such designations are part of the winemaker's contract with us. They ensure that we are getting a wine from their winery, made from grapes produced locally in their vineyard.

The interesting thing about place-identified wines is that they can be a complete mystery to the mass market of wine consumers. Wine store customers may recognize Pouilly-Fuissé or Chianti even if they do not know the grapes that are used. Some place names sell well on the mass market simply because they are so familiar. Worse yet, some wines will attract label-conscious consumers based simply on price. Those same consumers may skip a less well-known place-labeled wine even if it is their favorite wine varietal. So the place label may be our best friend or our worst enemy. Many place-identified wines may be at a disadvantage in the modern wine market because the place label outside most of Europe has given way to a peculiarly American invention: the varietal label.

The varietal label developed as a means of dealing with restrictions on place labeling. Prior to varietal labeling vintners used place labels without regard to the location of their vineyards. Ideally this was based on a match between the varietal used in the wine and the varietal used in the identified region. Less scrupulous vintners would use such labels indiscriminately. Any red wine might be labeled a Burgundy even if there wasn't a drop of wine from the region or from pinot noir grapes.

From a marketing perspective, the advent of regulations designed to protect place names were a coup for the vintners of well-known wine-producing regions. The regulations forced other vintners to adopt place labels that would mean nothing to the wine consumers of their day. Not surprisingly it is because of such regulations that we see the proliferation of varietals labeling. Labels based on varietals rather than places provide a means of marketing wine that stems from something consumers can readily understand. Personally, I don't mind browsing through a wine atlas in order to figure out the grape varietals in place-labeled wines. The majority of wine consumers are not so inclined. As such, varietals labeling helps winemakers bypass the issues involved in enforced place labeling.

THE ORIGINS OF CORPORATE WINE

Of all the information that might appear on a wine bottle, what will be absent is any corporate labeling. We could venture from bottle to bottle without a clue that their producers are all subsidiaries of the same large corporation. They simply do not put that kind of information on the label.

The involvement of big corporations in the wine industry is a natural outgrowth of the economic geography of the industry and part of a long evolutionary process that takes winemaking decisions away from individual vineyard owners and places them in the hands of major corporations. Unfortunately it may also change wine from being an expression of the uniqueness of a place to a homogenized corporate product. Although this does not have to be the case, it is hard to argue that the culture of wine is not tainted when wine is produced in facilities that look more like oil refineries than romantic Bordeaux châteaux.

When viewing winemaking as a business, there are a variety of problems that stand in the way of making a profit. First there are the environmental hazards that are inherent to any kind of agriculture. Periodic economic depressions can also pose risks for an industry that produces what is often viewed as a luxury item. Political problems between producer and consumer countries can also pose potential problems for an industry that has limited zones of production but an almost unlimited array of consumers. Regulations on wine sales and tariffs can negatively impact profits. Changing patterns of consumer preference can alter wine consumption or, in the case of the temperance movement, eliminate it almost entirely. These threats change the geography of the industry. Over time, they have led to wine becoming big business, and a multinational one at that.

The issue both geographically and economically is that the larger the enterprise the greater its resources and resilience in the face of hardship. An individual producer may be able to produce a great bottle of wine. However, that same producer may not be able to survive a few bad harvests or may not have the financial resources to keep pace with a changing marketplace. Shifting consumer preferences to new grape varietals may isolate the individual producer from the market if his or her land is not capable of producing those varietals. To protect themselves, individual producers may form cooperatives. In doing so they may specialize in the production of the grapes, leaving the more complex tasks of producing and marketing wine to other people. These seemingly small steps, viewed over time, lead to bigger and bigger concerns and to the rise of the multinational producers that we see today.

Consider the individual producer. If everything works well, he can produce a high-value crop that yields a high-quality and profitable wine. The existing producers may be able to put their profits into savings and reinvest in their product. If conditions are very good, new producers can enter the market, bringing new lands into grape production. More producers mean more competition. In a good market, this increase may simply mean that the profits are split among more producers. Unfortunately, for every economic boom there is a bust. There may be bad harvests, export problems, pest infestations, or any number of other things that cut into the profitability of wine production. If these conditions persist, marginal producers and/or those with limited resources may go bankrupt or be forced into growing other crops. The result is that there are good deals to be had on vineyards and wineries that are available to those who have the ability to make such purchases and to hold on to them until conditions improve. Larger producers with deeper pockets can snap up the best small vineyards and wineries, adding them to their inventories. At the end of the day, market downturns weed out small marginal producers, leading to larger wine concerns with greater land holdings. This process does not reverse itself during good markets. It simply reinforces the strength of the larger producers and their ability to withstand the next market decline.

If we look at the wine market as a global concern, the gulf between a producer that dominates a region's production and multinationals such as Fosters, Diageo, or Pernod-Ricard is not a large one. A large regional producer may still be at risk to hazards that affect its home region. Buying out smaller competitors within its home region may also become impractical as the cost of those purchases increase. These drawbacks provide an incentive to look outside the region for places that offer economic opportunity and protect against hazards specific to the producer's home region. This geographic diversification will often occur in tandem with market diversification. A company may move into the production of beer and spirits, diversifying its product line as well as the regions in which it operates. It may even branch out into business ventures in other arenas. A large wine producer in a single region may thus evolve into a multinational corporation with a variety of product lines within and beyond the alcoholic beverage industry. Likewise, big corporations may see the alcoholic beverage industry as a target as they diversify their portfolios.

The importance of large companies to the economic geography of the wine industry is also reflected in how wines reach local consumers. Throughout the history of the industry, there have been divisions between the production of wine, its transportation, and its sale. Unlike wine production, wine distribution has always included a significant corporate presence. Local networks of transportation, warehousing, and distribution may still operate independent of big corporations. This is especially true in beer, where local brewers may still distribute their product directly to nearby pubs and inns. For distribution networks that stretch long distances, there have always been middlemen and corporations. Consumers seem to be okay with that. It has nothing to do with the product. It just gets the wine to where we can buy it.

In some circles, to label a company a "multinational" is to vilify it. Where multinationals get their bad name has to do with blue-collar employment. There the multinationals have lots of options. It is the search for cheap factory labor and the export of production to the third world that makes many companies multinational. Ideally, the outsourcing of jobs to poor countries would become a stepping-stone for the economic advancement of those countries. The reality is that the countries to which the jobs are outsourced usually have no unions, no minimum wages, and few legal protections for labor. They likely are also lacking in the environmental protections that exist in the multinational's home country. Rather than making things better, the multinational milks the situation for its own benefit. Economic advancement would be counterproductive for the multinational, as this would increase their cost of doing business.

Alcohol producers are not that kind of multinational—not because they do not want to be, but because they produce a product that does not readily fit the traditional multinational model. The growth of alcohol multinationals is based on product diversification and profit seeking. The traditional multinational model expands upon these goals for industries that have significant labor requirements, use a lot of labor, and have high labor costs. Cost cutting and profit maximization lead these industries to seek out locations that allow them to minimize labor costs. For white-collar employment in management, research, and high-technology activities, multinationals have limited options. They can choose from a limited number of countries and locations that have such labor, and it seldom comes cheap.

The interesting thing about alcohol multinationals is that they do not seem to follow this model. This is due, at least in part, to the fact that the labor costs for alcohol producers are not as significant as in other industries. Also, a major accident of history is at work here. As discussed earlier, the process of fermentation tends to link wine production with the regions where grapes are grown. This limits the ability of big companies to seek out alternative production locations. Wine production takes place near vineyards and there is little that big corporations can do economically to change that.

It is in the link between wine production and vineyard location that we see how history has played an interesting trick on the wine industry. The countries that produce wine are some of the most expensive labor markets on earth. With a few exceptions the major wine-producing countries tend to be those that normally export low-skill jobs to the world's poor countries. This means that multinationals have to find other alternatives to lower labor costs. They do so not by exporting the jobs, but are forced to seek mechanized alternatives for the most labor-intensive parts of wine production. They also make use of cheap seasonal and immigrant labor to lower costs.

All in all, alcohol multinationals are just different. They are in it for the money, of course. They are not, however, in the same league as the multinationals that are capitalizing on third-world poverty. Consequently they do not have the same dire reputation as others of their kind. That said, big corporate involvement in the wine industry is not what most of us are looking for in our favorite beverage.

CHAMPAGNE

We have already discussed some of the regions that have distinctive processes for making wine. In particular, we talked about the wines of Madeira, Oporto, and Jerez. Champagne is another wine that is created through a variation on the basic process of winemaking. It is a different type of wine that has become synonymous with a place name. Then again, champagne is more than that. Champagne has transcended the wine label to become a status symbol. It is a must-have drink for celebrations and special occasions. Why is that? Is there something instinctive that makes us drink champagne on those occasions? Is a New Year's Eve party something less with a Riesling? Will a ship sink if it is christened with a cabernet sauvignon?

We can talk endlessly about champagne the wine. What can we say about Champagne the place? Champagne the place is a pretty region of river valleys near the cities of Reims and Épernay a few hours drive east of Paris. In terms of wine, it is simply a good region for growing and blending chardonnay, pinot noir, and pinot meunier grapes. It is similar to some parts of Burgundy. There is a lot of wine production in Champagne although its geographic extent is limited. The best production is from the hillsides eroded by the river Marne, where erosion has exposed thick layers of chalk that are buried elsewhere in the region. As a result, in some locations the soil is almost white. The exposed chalk makes for good wine-producing soil. As chalk is very easy to work with, the exposed layers are also great for carving out wine cellars. None of these things are unique to Champagne. So it is really the champagne that makes Champagne unique and important.

Depending on how your favorite wine store organizes its stock, there may be very little distinction between what is grouped under the "champagne" label. That is because the process or *méthode champenoise* that leads to the creation of all those wines is basically the same. The important thing is that they all start with a blend of different grapes. In champagne the combination is chardonnay, pinot noir, and pinot meunier. In other places the combination may be different. Blending alleviates seasonal variations in the quality of the grapes. It could be a high-rainfall year, or a dry sunny year, or a cold windy year. With blending the consistency of the overall taste is what matters. Blending allows for the use of grapes that would not make for the best vintage wines. It also allows the champagne houses to use grapes from vineyards that would not be ideal for vintage wine production.

The *méthode champenoise* that produces champagne is a relatively recent development as far as the wine industry is concerned. It requires the kinds of airtight seals that were not possible prior to glass-bottling. By conducting part of the fermentation process within airtight containers, the gases produced by fermentation are trapped. This is what gives champagne its bubbles. In wood barrels these gases would escape and champagne would have no fizz. The accumulation of gases from the fermentation process increases pressure within the bottles. Prior to the development of good-quality bottling-making techniques, the pressure resulted in much bottle breakage, worker injuries, and loss of champagne. Today the quality of the bottles is such that it takes a great deal of effort to break them, though it is still important to exercise some care when releasing the corks on champagne bottles.

The use of bottle aging also traps the sediment (marc) that derives from the fermentation process. By storing the bottles at an angle with the cork at the bottom, and by rotating the bottles through time, the sediment collects in the neck of the bottle. This process (called remuage) is important if we want clear and sediment-free champagne. Experienced handlers can then open the bottles and remove the sediment without it going back into suspension in the wine. In this process, called degorgement, the bottles are opened and the sediment removed. The bottles are then topped off and corked for storage and eventual sale. As with other variations on wine production, there is nothing that would necessarily prevent someone from doing this outside Champagne. It is only a form of production that has become so entwined with the place that the process carries the place name.

So why associate champagne with the big business of wine? The reason is that behind many of the world's great champagne labels there are major corporate entities. And not just big beverage corporations, but hotel chains, luxury-product companies, investment companies, and banks. This begs the question: Why would champagne be a product in demand by big corporations? The prestige of the product is one reason. This is especially true for beverage companies. For companies that sell luxury goods to a high-end clientele the ownership of a champagne house would be a natural sideline for their business. The consistency of champagne sales would be another reason that corporations might own a champagne house, although the quality of such an investment may not be what it once was, given the number of champagne producers now in the marketplace.

Even if champagne houses are not owned by big corporations, they may act like it. Champagne producers invest in businesses linked to their product. They sponsor sports linked by status and lifestyle to the people who would most likely drink their champagne. They also aggressively market their products. For most of us, champagne is a drink that we associate with important occasions. The people who make champagne work very hard to make sure that we don't forget that. So while champagne may be a wine, a place, and a method, we should not forget that it is also a very big business.

Champagne reflects a new role for wine as a multinational product, status symbol, and a sign of wealth. But for those of us who love wine, there is a lot more to champagne than big business. Champagne is good wine. As such, champagne is a reflection of the place, history, and people who produce it. We may sometimes lose sight of those links in all the champagne hype, but they are there waiting for us if we care to look for them.

Chapter 17

LOCALISM AND WINE
TOURISM

Most farms are not high on the agenda for tourists. Fields of corn, barns full of stalls for dairy cows, sheds of giant wheat harvesters, muddy tractors, and irrigation equipment do not excite the imaginations of most folks. Viticulture is agriculture, just like a dairy farm. So what makes a winery or a vineyard worth a visit while a dairy farm does not even merit a second look as we drive down the road?

Visitors to a vineyard or a winery do not think about them as industrial concerns. Even if a winery is nothing more than a factory for processing grapes, this is not what is in the mind of the wine tourist. Industrial heritage tourism is all about visits to factories and mines, where one visits an old factory to see the machinery, or dons gear and rides down into the depths of a coal mine. That is not to say that there is anything wrong with those types of tourist venues. In fact, there is probably nothing that my kids would love more than riding a tram deep into a mine so that they can run around in the dark wearing miner's helmets.

Visiting a winery is not industrial heritage tourism. What makes it different is that it is all about the love of place. It is about taste and history and culture. Even though it is a factory, a winery is a place that stresses our link to nature and encourages us to learn about it. While it consists of agricultural fields and a barn, a winery is also much more than that.

TOURISM AND WINE

Tourism is a very interesting subject for geographers. As an example of the geography of economy, tourism raises questions about supply, demand, and the spatial impacts of the industry. Tourism is also about people traveling for sights and experiences different from those at home. Through this definition of tourism we concern ourselves with an entirely different geography. We enter into discussions of places and landscapes, the movement of people and the routes that they take, their experiences and discoveries, and the education that comes with travel.

What is it that we study in tourism? A good deal of research on tourism is focused on tourists themselves. Geographers are very interested in where people go, why they go there, and what they do. We study the motivations for tourism and how they lead to travel decisions. We might take a look at why someone would want to visit a wine region. Moreover, we can look at how they choose which wine region(s) to visit. What would motivate them to visit Napa versus Burgundy, Tuscany versus the Mosel Valley? Is it money? Time? Culture? Or something else entirely? Will they take a guided tour or will they bike around independently? Will they visit wineries or take wine and cooking classes at local restaurants? Will they travel by airplane, boat, car, or train to get to the wine region? Are wine tourists more likely to stay in four-star hotels, small B&Bs, or at youth hostels? What motivates tourists to return to the same destinations?

Beyond the questions that deal with choice and the logistics of tourism, we are also keenly interested in what people learn through tourism. Tourism can be a tremendous learning experience. It can shape the way people think about and see other cultures. By immersing ourselves in a place and its people we can learn in days what it might take months to communicate in a classroom. As such, tourism can be an extraordinary tool for learning about the world around us.

Even if the tourism experiences are negative, it is important that we understand them. Tourism is a very competitive industry, one that puts food on the table for a great many people. For the good of both the tourists and the people who make their living from tourism it is important to understand why someone would have a negative experience. It is a form of problem solving. If we can figure out what went wrong and why, we can fix the problem for the next group of tourists. If not, there may not be a next group of tourists.

There is another side of tourism, which we sometimes forget in our travels: the economic, social, and environmental impacts that we as travelers have on the places that we visit. In all of these there is a benefit and a cost to tourism because for every instance where the environment has been used to attract tourists there are instances of tourism leading to environmental degradation. For every local merchant who makes money off of tourism there are others who find tourists to be intrusive and a pain to deal with.

So what makes wine the subject matter of tourism? To understand the answer to that question we need to look at some of the motivations for wine tourism. Wine tourism is an escape from the routine of our daily lives. It is a wonderful adventure. If we want to experience that adventure in the slow lane, wine tourism can be a form of relaxation and a means to unwind. It can also be a source of exercise and a physical stimulus if we prefer a more active approach to the travel. Wine tourism can also be an intellectual exercise, stimulating the mind as well as the body.

Such motivations for wine tourism are not all that different from those behind any other form of tourism, and could also apply to museum-based tours, spa retreats, and river cruises. What differentiates wine tourism is what we are paying for. Obviously we are paying for all of the normal "stuff" of tourism: the journey, the accommodations, the activities, and the things that we spend money on while we are traveling. More than that, in wine tourism we are paying for a rural ideal. We are buying a connection to the earth and to the people who make their living from it. Maybe that is why huge corporate wineries do not fire our imaginations. In a sense we are buying some of the local culture in wine tourism. In an urban setting we might be able to see some of the local culture and experience a connection to the places we visit. The problem is that so much in modern cities is homogenized western urbanism. Even if the language is different and the people look and dress in a fashion that is different from home, the fact is that big cities have an awful lot in common.

Wine tourism gets tourists off of the beaten path. That is not to say that there is anything wrong with the beaten path. When I am in Paris I brave the crowds and visit the Louvre. I wait in line and venture up the Eiffel Tower as far as my fear of heights will allow me. I wander through the Musée d'Orsay, Notre Dame, and all of the other major tourism venues. The problem is that in doing so I never really need to step outside my comfort zone. I never have to speak French, interact with the locals, or immerse myself in the local culture.

The same cannot be said for most wine tourism. Except for a few heavily traveled regions, wine tourism takes us out into the countryside where tourists are more the exception than the rule. It takes us to places where commuter trains and tour buses do not go, to places where people may know a lot about wine, but not how to speak English. What it really does is to take us to places where we are individuals, not part of the endless procession of people waiting for the elevator to go up the Eiffel Tower. For a small, out-of-the-way winery, we may be the only visitors it will have all day. In this way, wine tourism is more of a challenge and an active intellectual exercise. We can immerse ourselves and have an experience that is unique to us. Anyone can visit the Louvre and experience seeing the Mona Lisa. How many people can experience meeting "the locals" and muddling their way through a foreign language as they describe the great things about their communities and their wine?

What makes for good wine tourism? Thankfully there is no one answer for that. The world is full of many different kinds of people, each of whom with their own likes and dislikes. What motivates one person, such as biking through beautiful vineyards at harvest time, may be a turnoff to another. The good thing about wine tourism is that it can offer a variety of experiences for tourists to choose from. As long as our idea of travel is more than spending a week lying on the beach at an all-inclusive resort, there is going to be something in wine tourism to motivate our interests.

Many kinds of wine tourism are available. There are traditional guided tours. For the more independent-minded tourist there are self-guided tours by car. For those who are looking for a slower pace but greater physical challenges there are hiking and cycling tours. All wine tourism involves some kind of educational activity. For those who really want to emphasize the educational side of tourism there are opportunities to take part in cooking tours or academic programs linked to wine. Wine tourism can be a major focus of travel, or it can be a fun addition to other kinds of tourism. The great thing about wine tourism is that every wine region is a new experience waiting to happen, with its own wines, its own history, its own landscapes, and its own culture. Even if we return to a region we visited earlier we can alter the experience each time. We can visit during a different season, select different wineries, or go to non-wine-related sites within that region. By altering our travel, each visit becomes a new experience and a new learning opportunity.

CENTRAL ITALY

In a discussion of wine, most books typically focus on Italy rather early on, because Italy is one of the world's biggest wine producers, and is a great place to grow grapes and produce wine. With very few exceptions, wine can be produced almost everywhere in Italy.

I have saved Italy for the end of this book, not to slight Italy or its wines, but because it is exemplary of wine tourism in all its various forms. In Italy we can see and experience many different kinds of wine tourism. Because I personally associate Italy with tourism and wine, I have saved the best for last.

Italy is a fantastic place for producing wine. There is enough climatic variation to make it possible to grow many different grape varietals. In a general sense, Italy's climate ranges from cool and damp in the north to hot and dry in the south. Of course, there is a lot more to it than that. Most of Italy is surrounded by the Mediterranean and Adriatic seas. These water bodies moderate the country's climate. At the same time, the mountain ranges (the Alps and Dolomites) that form Italy's northern border prevent the worst of Europe's winter weather from reaching south into the peninsula. By contrast, the mountains that form the spine of Italy create localized climatic variations, microclimates, suited to many different grape varietals.

Even grape varietals that prefer cooler climates can find a suitable location somewhere in Italy. What this means is that wine production is omnipresent. Regions that are not known for wine or do not have an official designation, may still be home to plenty of wine producers who provide wine for local consumers. The result is that anywhere we go in Italy there will be some sort of opportunity to visit and experience Italian wineries and vineyards.

Ironically, what makes Italy a great place for wine tourism is all of the other tourist destinations that the country has to offer. The myriad of wonderful cities, historic sites, religious centers, and great museums only adds to the allure of wine tourism in Italy. In dynamic regions where it is literally impossible to do everything in a single visit, tour operators can create a mix of experiences in every tour, and it's likely that tourists will come back to a region to experience what they couldn't during their first trip. If there are more museums to see, more historic sites to visit, and more wineries and vineyards to tour, then it is much easier to see repeat business. A visit to the wine regions of Campania can be combined with a tour of Naples and Pompeii. The Veneto offers up its wineries to those who have the time to venture beyond Venice. Lombardia has wineries waiting for visitors who want to take a brief day trip from Lake Como or Lake Maggiore. Even in Rome there are nearby wine regions waiting for those brave spirits who are willing to jump in a car and tackle the city's traffic.

Up and down the boot of Italy there are wine regions within striking distance of almost any place a tourist would care to go. Of course, the pinnacle of Italian wine tourism is in Tuscany. Tuscany has some of Italy's best wines. In addition, Tuscany offers tourists a tremendous amount of history, including the city of Florence, with its artistic, historic, and architectural wonders, and Pisa, with its leaning tower. It also has smaller but no less impressive cities such as Siena and San Gimignano. In Tuscany we can take a tour, drive, hike, or bike. We can rent a villa, stay in a four-star hotel, or in a romantic B&B. We can spend our vacation in the vineyards or just see one or two vineyards on an afternoon excursion. It is all in Tuscany.

You could spend a lifetime getting to know Italian wines and their geography. The diversity of peoples and environments in Italy is such that almost any wine can be found there. Consequently, Italy is a great place to explore the geography of wine whether it is in the bottles that the country produces or in the places that Italians call home.

Chapter 18

WHERE WINE TAKES ME

$\mathcal{F}\!\!\mathit{or}$ me, the appreciation and love of wine goes beyond the wine itself. Wine is an expression of places and people. That is the experience I get having a glass of wine. In my opinion, wine is as much about place and experience as it is about taste and appearance. And so, in closing this book, I would like to share with you the wine places and experiences that I come back to again and again. This is personal. It is also a reflection of some of the things that geographers see and experience in wine and the places that produce it.

To find a wine experience that relates as much to history as to geography, it would be hard to pick a better region than the southern Rhône Valley in France. The wines of the region have a strong connection to the history of the Roman Empire as it can still be seen in the architectural heritage of the towns of Nîmes and Arles, and in Avignon from which the popes of the fourteenth century ruled Christendom. Admittedly, it is a place I have not been to in more than twenty years, but given the money and the time, it is definitely the place I would choose to go.

Geographically, the southern Rhône Valley is as interesting as its history. Climatically, the region is very different from

France north of the Alps and Massif Central. In spring and fall the region is affected by the mistral winds sweeping down from the mountains. In summer it is buffeted by warm air from northern Africa. The central focus of the region is the city of Avignon. From there, the Rhône River spills out over a large delta on its way to the Mediterranean. To the west of the delta is the town of Nîmes in Languedoc. To the east is the town of Arles, at the westernmost edge of Provence. Within the delta there is the Camargue, with its castles, wetlands, nature preserves, and unique culture. Every two or three years the riders of the Tour de France are challenged by the ride up Mont Ventoux. More important, every fall the rocky hillside and valley vineyards produce some of the world's great red wines.

For the Romans this part of Gaul (modern-day France) was as close to home in its climate and geology as anywhere else they would find in their conquests. So when the Romans arrived they were able to transplant their culture and their wine. As this area remained part of the empire for a very long time, the Roman influence was able to soak in and become part of the local culture. Unlike in other parts of the empire, when the Romans left their legacy remained. It is this historical imprint that continues to impress me after twenty years. I still have strong memories of drinking wine at cafés next door to Roman structures dating back millennia. Through the heritage of the region's wines and the architecture of its cities you can feel a tangible connection to history. You can easily imagine that two thousand years ago people sat in the same place and drank the same wines.

The things that make the southern Rhône and Provence unique, and set it apart from the rest of France, were what drew artists to the region. The dry air allows light to more easily pass through the atmosphere. There is the warmth of the Mediterranean climate and the contrast between the blues of the sea coast against the reds of the roof tiles, tans of the rocky soils, greens of the palms, olives, and grapevines, with the seasonal purples (if lavender is in bloom) of the mainland. I am no artist, but I can appreciate the inspiration that the region held for artists such as van Gogh, Picasso, and Chagall.

The artistry of the southern Rhône as far as wine is concerned comes with the region's great red wines. Grenache grapes here are traditionally blended with Syrah (called Shiraz if it was produced in an English-speaking wine region), and a wide variety of lesser-known local varietals. The combinations are dictated by climate and soils and by the traditions of the vintners in the region. Between Avignon and the town of Orange, the vintners of Châteauneuf-du-Pape (roughly translated as "new home of the pope") are still producing the complex red-wine blends that graced the tables of the popes seven hundred years ago. For those occasions that do not merit the cost of Châteauneuf-du-Pape, the southern Rhône produces very good Côtes du Rhône, and Côtes du Rhône Villages reds with combinations similar to their more expensive neighbor. You can get a taste of what the climate and soils of the region produce no matter what your pocketbook allows.

To appreciate wine and its geography the best option is often the one closest to home. For me, home is Connecticut. While New England does not immediately bring to mind fine wines, wine production here has a significant history. In New England, wine production dates back to the colonial period. The wine industry that we see today is, however, of a very recent origin. It is also an industry that mirrors its setting quite nicely. The wineries are not large nor are they industrial. They are small and quaint. Part boutique and part agriculture, they quite nicely complement the summer tourist towns and seaside resorts that dot the shoreline. That said, these wineries are more than charming tourist traps. They produce some very nice vintages.

The climate of New England is not ideal for wine production. Winters can be miserably cold and snowy. However, the impact of the open waters of the Atlantic Ocean is enough to make parts of the coastline reasonable for growing grapes. That is why the best grape growing in the region can be found where the influence of the ocean is most pronounced—on the North Fork of Long Island (the northernmost peninsula, or "fork" on the island's east end). In winter the winds are warmed ever so slightly as they pass over the open water of Long Island Sound, and in summer they are cooled by the water. This lengthens the growing season and makes for pretty good conditions on the North Fork. On the north mainland shore of Long Island Sound, conditions are not quite as good, but there are locations where the effects of the Atlantic, good soil, and protection from the northern winds are sufficient to allow for wine production.

What makes viticulture popular and profitable in this area is as much about people as it is about microclimates. The Northeast is the most densely populated part of the United States. The places producing wine are also those that attract hordes of tourists throughout the summer months. As a result, there are a lot of people to sell wine to. For the locals, the wineries can make for fun day trips out of New York, Boston, Hartford, or Providence.

For the tourists, the wineries are part of what draws them to the coast. Wineries have become part of the itinerary.

The relationship between wineries and tourism has a geographic, economic, and aesthetic impact on the wineries. The population and the demand for land along the coast make buying property an expensive proposition. Therefore, most wineries are not large, the exceptions being in areas that are not prime real estate for tourism. This is why wineries line the North Fork of Long Island and not the heavily touristed South Fork. There are only a few South Fork wineries, and they are located far inland of the Hamptons and that area's expensive seaside homes and summer resorts.

Being tourist destinations, the look and feel of the wineries is important. Whether it is day-trippers or seasonal tourists, visitors to the region do not want to visit wineries that look like factories. They do not want vineyards that look like farms. Visitors to the region want a look and feel of a rustic, romantic winery. It does not matter whether the styles are French provincial, Newport, or rural eclectic; for wineries that cater to the tourist trade, appearance is exceptionally important.

As wine has grown in popularity, so has the number of wineries within southern New England. Even where grapes have not been readily available, wineries in the region have sprung up to feed the demand. Some have done so by importing grapes, others by using grape substitutes. For the wineries on or near Cape Cod, the cranberry bogs have provided just such an alternative. Because the same environments that produce great cranberries are simply not conducive to most grape varietals, local vintners use either cranberries or imported grapes in the production of their wine. While the very idea of cranberry wine may be sacrilegious to some, it makes for an interesting regional twist on the wines that are available here.

What also intrigues me about the wineries of the Northeast is the sense of discovery that they bring. The wines produced here rarely appear in local wine stores. Most of them require some effort to find. The same can be said for some of the region's wineries. They are small, sometimes on back roads, and off the beaten path. This sense of discovery also extends to first vintages. With all of the new wineries in southern New England, opportunities arise to taste a first vintage here that you do not find in most established winemaking regions, which makes the wines of this region a lot of fun.

One of the things I like best about wine is its ability to take us places. It does not have to be actual travel. It can just be the sensation that when you are drinking wine you are transported to another place. For me, wine takes me to Vienna. It matters little that I am drinking wine that comes from someplace else. When my mind starts to drift, usually after the second glass of anything, Vienna and its nearby wine regions is where it drifts to.

Wine in this part of Europe is not a succession of vineyards and wineries as far as the eye can see. It is produced in small vineyards intermixed with other forms of agriculture. In the valleys it is mixed with wheat and vegetable farming as well as dairying, and in the hills with woodlands. This creates a visually appealing landscape where each vineyard has an interesting geographical explanation. The proximity of Vienna to wine regions in Austria, Slovakia, and Hungary means that there is a variety of cultures to be experienced along with the wine. Moreover, wine here does not attract lines of tour buses and tourists by the hundreds. These are places where you can believe that you are discovering something new. For me that makes it special.

Even if you go to Vienna but never venture beyond the city, you can get a glimpse of Austria's wine culture. Vineyards in the northern suburbs of Vienna are readily accessible by city bus. You can walk through the hillside vineyards down to the *heurigen* (wine taverns) in the valley. It is a bit touristy, but if you can ignore that, it is a nice primer for what Austrian wine country has to offer.

When I travel I like to rent a car and get out into the countryside. From Vienna a nice day out on the roads will take you to the wine regions of Weinviertel, Kamptal, Kremstal, and Wachau, northwest of Vienna. I like Grüner Veltliner wines, the light white wines that are produced almost everywhere in the region. The rolling wooded hills, quaint towns, and well-tended farms are such that every turn of the road presents another splendid landscape. In each town you find friendly people as well as family-style restaurants that dish out hearty portions of Wiener schnitzel and *erdapfelsalat* (potato salad), all of which makes for a really memorable experience.

If you do not have a car, Danube River cruises out of Vienna allow you to appreciate the region and its wines from the comfort of the water. Most of the cruises stop at the market town of Krems. The town's walls, its maze of side streets, and its cathedral perched high over the river makes it a highlight of the trip. For the price of a full-day cruise you can venture beyond Krems through the picturesque Wachau valley. Assuming that you like picturesque landscapes dotted with small towns and hilltop castles, the valley is definitely worth the extra time spent on the boat. In this way, the geography of wine can be appreciated from the water.

After a day or two traveling around northern Austria, the Neusiedlersee wine regions south of Vienna make for a nice change of pace. The Neusiedlersee is a large shallow lake on the Austria–Hungary border. The lake is large enough—around three miles wide and eighteen miles long—to create a microclimate capable of supporting a diversity of grape varietals. This is not just another valley planted with Grüner Veltliner. The surrounding vineyards and wineries are small and produce a variety of wines, and there are many little discoveries to be made. In past years, the trip around the lake would have been a short one, ending at the Hungarian border. With the end of the Cold War and the entry of Hungary into the EU, circling the lake is no longer a problem. You can enter Hungary, taste their wines, and see what fifty years of communism meant for the people of the region. The trip around the lake is also quite nice as an introduction to bike touring. The virtually flat terrain allows for a comfortable afternoon of low-impact biking and wine tasting.

The Little Carpathian Wine Route in Slovakia is another great day trip from Vienna. As with the route around Neusiedlersee, this would have been an impossible trip during the Cold War. It takes you into the hills which farther to the east become the Carpathian Mountains. The wine route starts north of Bratislava, about an hour's drive from Vienna. For wine tourists this is about as far off the beaten track as you can get. The route takes you through the small towns of Rača, Modra, and Častá, and their surrounding vineyards. The small wineries on the route produce Rieslings, Müller-Thurgau, and other cold-tolerant grape varietals. Tolerance to cold is an absolute necessity as this is about as far northeast as you can go in Europe and still reliably produce grapes. More than the climate and the varieties of wine, the real experience of the route is Slovakia itself. The people, culture, food (these are the places to fill up on sauerkraut and goulash), and the impact of five decades of communism are all there. After pointing and smiling through a few winery visits (I do not speak Slovak or German), the capstone experience of the trip for me is Bratislava. An evening in the old town of Bratislava is more than just a pit stop on the way back to Vienna. The old town is alive with restaurants and music (jazz seems to be quite popular throughout the region), all cast against a background of historic architecture dating from the seventeenth, eighteenth, and nineteenth centuries, making Bratislava quite a memorable place and well worth a side trip from Vienna.

I hope that you all have your own wine places. If not, I would encourage you to go out and explore them, either in books, on-line, or in person. And do not worry if your wine places are different from other people's. That is the nice thing about our subject. Behind the science and social science there is a great deal that is personal. It allows us to raise a glass of wine and see in it so much more than just wine. So here's to the geography in your next glass!

APPENDIX

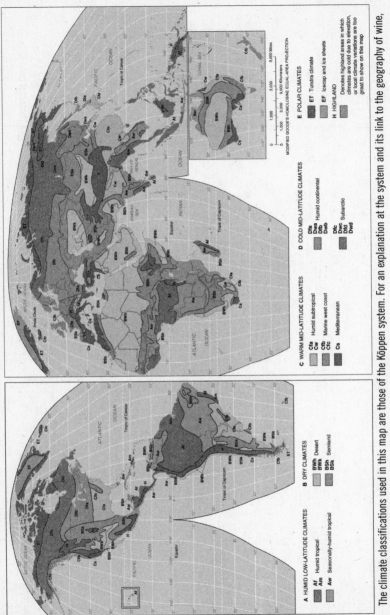

A HUMID LOW-LATITUDE CLIMATES
Af Humid tropical
Am
Aw Seasonally-humid tropical

B DRY CLIMATES
BWh Desert
BWk
BSh Semiarid
BSk

C WARM MID-LATITUDE CLIMATES
Cfa Humid subtropical
Cwa
Cfb Marine west coast
Cfc
Cs Mediterranean

D COLD MID-LATITUDE CLIMATES
Dfa Humid continental
Dwa
Dfb
Dwb
Dfc Subarctic
Dwc
Dfd
Dwd

E POLAR CLIMATES
ET Tundra climate
EF Icecap and ice sheets
H HIGHLAND
Denotes highland areas in which climates are cold due to elevation, or local climate variations are too great to show on this map

MODIFIED GOODE'S HOMOLOSINE EQUAL-AREA PROJECTION

0   1,000   2,000   3,000 Miles
0 1,000 2,000 3,000 Kilometers

The climate classifications used in this map are those of the Köppen system. For an explanation at the system and its link to the geography of wine, please see the chart on the next page and the material in chapter 3.

Climates	Most Well-Known Grape Varietals	Representative Wine Regions
Continental/Marine West Coast	Red—pinot noir. White—gewürtzraminer and Riesling	Burgundy, Champagne, Mosel Valley, the Northeastern United States, and colder locations in Oregon and Washington
Marine West Coast	Red—cabernet sauvignon, gamay, merlot, pinot noir, zinfandel. White—chardonnay, Riesling, sauvignon blanc, trebbiano	Bordeaux, colder locations in Napa and Sonoma, Chilean wine regions, inland wine regions in New South Wales, and warmer locations in Oregon and Washington
Marine West Coast/ Mediterranean	Red—cabernet sauvignon, gamay, merlot, Sangiovese, zinfandel. White—chardonnay, sauvignon blanc, trebbiano	Northern Italy, coastal locations in southeastern Australia, and warmer locations in Napa and Sonoma
Mediterranean	Red—Barbera, grenache, Sangiovese, Syrah/Shiraz. White—chenin blanc, Palomino	Chianti, southern France, most of Spain and Portugal, South African wine regions
Mediterranean/Desert fringe	Red—Barbera, grenache, Syrah/Shiraz. White—Palomino	Parts of Spain, wine regions near the Great Australian Desert, the Central Valley of California, southern and eastern parts of the Mediterranean basin

The climates listed are those used in the Köppen system and on the climate map on the preceding page. The relationships between climates, grape varietals, and regions are generalized. Microclimatic differences as well as issues of soils and topography can alter the environments so as to allow for the use of other grape varietals. Many other lesser-known or less-common grape varietals are available. Some of these may be important to wine production in particular regions. Cultural and economic concerns may also influence the pattern of grape varietals used. Some of the grape varietals identified have broad tolerances for variations in climate and soils. Even so, wine produced from those grapes may be very different depending on environmental conditions.

FURTHER READING

It seems there are always more wine books coming onto the market. But rather than going wild buying books, I tend to come back to the same favorites again and again. Here is my personal short list.

Hugh Johnson, *Story of Wine*, London: Octopus Publishing Group, 2004. As far as the history of wine is concerned this is number one. Rather than following strict chronologies, Johnson weaves a series of historical wine stories. For more than just the content and approach, I like Johnson's work because of the quality of the writing. That is also why I would suggest any wine book written by Jancis Robinson.

Tim Unwin, *Wine and the Vine*, London: Taylor & Francis, 1991. Also wonderfully rich in historical wine stories.

Hugh Johnson and Jancis Robinson, *The World Atlas of Wine*, London: Octopus Publishing Group, 5th edition, 2006.

Oz Clarke, *Oz Clarke's New Wine Atlas*, New York: Harcourt, 2002. This and *The World Atlas of Wine* have excellent mapping.

Robert White, *Soils for Fine Wine*, New York: Oxford University Press, 2003; and James Wilson, *Terroir: The Role of Geology, Climate, and Culture in the Making of French Wines*, Berkeley: University of California Press, 1999. Both of these are good references on the environmental science of wine, packed with information on wine, soils, and geology.

Albert Julius Winkler, et al., *General Viticulture*, Berkeley: University of California Press, 1975, is as good as any textbook on the subject.

INDEX

PHOTO CREDITS